In Vitro:
My Journey
Through the World
of
IVF

In Vitro:
My Journey
Through the World
of

An Inconvenient Truth about
In Vitro Fertilization

Anastasia Sputnik

iUniverse LLC
Bloomington

IN VITRO: MY JOURNEY THROUGH THE WORLD OF IVF
An Inconvenient Truth about In Vitro Fertilization

iUniverse books may be ordered through booksellers or by contacting:

iUniverse LLC
1663 Liberty Drive
Bloomington, IN 47403
www.iuniverse.com
1-800-Authors (1-800-288-4677)

ISBN: 978-1-4917-0447-9 (sc)
ISBN: 978-1-4917-0448-6 (e)

Library of Congress Control Number: 2013915169

Printed in the United States of America

iUniverse rev. date: 11/26/2013

CONTENTS

Part I
SEVEN YEARS OF IVF TREATMENTS

Part II
CONCLUSIONS AND ADVICE

To my born and unborn babies

PREFACE

I am a woman who, over a period of seven years, underwent in vitro fertilization treatments fifteen separate times. (Throughout this book, in vitro fertilization will be referred to as IVF).

This book started as my simple chronicle and collection of thoughts during the first years of my journey through the world of IVF. Throughout that time, I gained a tremendous amount of knowledge and experience as a result of many years of engaging in the different methods of assisted reproductive technologies (ART). I then decided to expand this book from just a chronicle of my experiences, thoughts, and feelings, into a tool to help others. I wanted to turn my failure into other women's and couples' success. I felt, and I still feel, that if children are born thanks to my book, all my battles and suffering will not be in vain.

Motivation for writing this book came when I realized that my IVF story, together with all the lessons I learned throughout my IVF battle, should not be wasted, but rather passed on to the other women and couples undergoing ART, in order to help them overcome their fertility problems—or at least give them some hope, inspiration, and encouragement to proceed (and finally succeed!), or to choose an alternative path.

Although I wanted to share my experiences honestly and openly, I had no intention of writing the book as a collection of essays or poetry that reflected only emotions. I wanted my book to be a well-organized presentation of information and discoveries about IVF, including my own conclusions and advice for women and couples undergoing similar experiences and traveling a similar path. The content in this book can help women and couples at different stages of infertility: those just diagnosed and embarking on IVF, those already going through IVF, those experiencing what is known as secondary infertility, and those dealing with terminating IVF (IVF closure) and finding a way to move on. In addition, this book can be a useful source of information about fertility for younger women and couples who have not yet begun IVF, but who, misinformed by the media, may easily end up starting IVF. I wish a book like this had existed when I started with IVF, and even afterward, when I was already in IVF, during my late thirties and early forties. However, I would have gained the most from such a book if I'd read it when I was in my late twenties and early thirties, so that I would have learned about fertility/infertility and the real capabilities and limits of ART procedures.

While writing this book, I felt as if I knew you, my future readers: Women (most likely) who have a lot in common with me. We share a destiny of going through the frustrations of infertility, with all its suffering, pain, uncertainty, and disappointment. We went from happy, fulfilled women to insecure, nervous, and superstitious women; from cool and good-looking women, to overweight, hypersensitive, hormone-pumped creatures. We went from having financial security, to living with a huge amount of debt on credit cards and loans. We went from having great marriages, to living in frustrating, even bullying, relationships with our partners; from living "happily ever after," "until death do us apart," to separation or divorce—all because we could not have a child or more children. I wanted to share my story with you—my friends by means of our shared experience—to give you some valuable information based on my experience, hoping that you will benefit from the wisdom I gained through my IVF battle, hoping to somehow ease your struggle to have a baby or more babies. I wanted to offer encouragement and support, to emphasize how important it is to be persistent, to advise how essential it is to have a Plan B in place from the very beginning (which, out of all the lessons I learned, is probably the most important or at least one of the most important). I also wanted to prepare you, emotionally and practically, for all the difficulties encountered during IVF; I wanted to reach out to those of you already in IVF, who are likely experiencing despair and depression, to let you know that you are not alone. But rather than mourning over the shared destiny of my fellow IVF participants, I wanted to offer a more practical approach, filled with information and advice, and in some instances, to just simply pass along the history of my fertility treatments and experiences, allowing you to draw your own conclusions.

Another reason I wrote this book was to expose some misinformation and misconceptions about fertility, infertility, and IVF in general. The media has spread much of this misinformation, which, in my opinion has already negatively impacted women, couples, and families; in the future, I believe these misconceptions will have even more serious, and even fatal, consequences. Thus, I felt obliged to disclose my discoveries throughout my battle with infertility and course of IVF. Even though I was deeply involved in IVF, I was nevertheless misinformed and misled. Because I was insufficiently educated about IVF, I had a lot of incorrect perceptions during the early stages of treatment, not to mention during the years prior to embarking on IVF. For all these reasons, I envision this book as an enlightening guide, not only for women and couples already involved in IVF, but also for the new generation of women around the planet, most of whom are not well educated about fertility and the capabilities and limitations of IVF—again, caused by the false information, incorrect interpretations, exaggerations, and general misconceptions spread by the media.

Throughout this book, I have intentionally not discussed the joys of motherhood, striving to keep my daughter "invisible," out of compassion for the women reading the book who have not yet had children and/or cannot have their own biological children.

Also, I wish to share that if I could turn back time, I definitely would have tried to start a family earlier in life. To me, there is no greater gift than a child, and for that gift, I would trade everything else in life: money, career, status, love, etc. Simply put, having a child is better than not having one—with or without a man; married or not married; divorced, separated, etc.; naturally or through IVF.

By the time I finished writing this book, I was forty-seven years old. Unfortunately, my "infertility story" is not yet finished. It will never be finished, because my entire life was marked by it, and always will be. My daughter will soon celebrate her tenth birthday. Her birth was, and always will be, the happiest and most important milestone of my life.

My story is for all of you reading this who share the same pain, despair, and challenges that I faced. I wish you luck on your own journeys. May this book help you remember that you are not alone.

ACKNOWLEDGMENTS

Limited number of people helped me during the years I went through IVF.

I would like to thank to my mother and sister, who followed the course of my infertility treatments, showing their continuous hope and support. They were also sad for the situation I was in. My mother, as a retired doctor understood well the amounts and types of hormonal stimulation I was getting through IVF treatments and she was concerned for the impacts and risks of hormonal stimulation on my body, mind and general health.

I would like to thank to my best childhood friend. Despite the fact that during the time of my life with IVF we lived in different continents and that we hadn't seen each other for couple of years, she was still the closest person to me. Through the frequent e-mail correspondence, she shared the hopes and disappointments that I faced throughout the numerous infertility treatments and especially during the period of IVF closure. She always expressed her love and care, her concerns and best wishes, cheered me up, helped me de-stress, and even helped me introduce some humor into the situation.

I would like to thank my stepmother who loves me and worries about me as if I were her own child. She encouraged me to write this book. She was excited to be the first to proof-read my book and I got from her valuable remarks and advice.

I would also like to thank my female colleague at work, who was always the first to hear the news from the clinic, continually open to hearing all the details, and ready to offer ongoing encouragement and empathy.

I wish I could thank my late father, who was so close to me and helped me so much, especially throughout the most difficult time of my entire life: the years of IVF closure, when I was enduring not only the painful acceptance of the reality that my second child would never be born, but also a very painful and stressful time in my marriage. My father provided strong love, care, understanding, and support, and he helped me to preserve my life, health, and values. He encouraged me to be a strong and loving mother for my daughter, despite the stress I was going through in my marriage. He was the closest person in the whole world to me during those final years of IVF, and we were both happy for that strong bond.

Despite the turbulences in my marriage throughout the final years of IVF, and the great suffering I went through, I still want to thank my husband: we made this journey together. He had to give up on his personal dream of a big family, just as I did. We both will carry that loss in our souls for the rest of our lives.

Most of my thanks go to my daughter. She motivated me and made all the years of struggling to have a second baby more bearable.

Finally, I also give special thanks to the fertility clinics and their doctors, nurses, and other clinical staff. Thank you for all your work, the services you provide, your research, discoveries, development, and successes. Thank you for existing!

INTRODUCTION

The standard opening sentence in many books is: "any similarity to real life is coincidental." This book is the opposite: the entire book is based on a real life; it is almost like a diary of going through fifteen fertility treatments for a period of seven years. I wish that were not the case; or at least I wish that I were just a curious reader of this book, not the author. Unfortunately, this book is the true story of what my husband and I, and our family, went through during our IVF journey.

I am not the first woman in the world who underwent many years of IVF procedures; however, I am one of the first to share valuable information and details, as well as the hidden truths and painful consequences of undergoing IVF. My experience as an IVF patient who went through many years of intensive and invasive IVF treatments in different clinics shows the IVF industry from the new perspective: that of a very involved and experienced patient who learned a lot of the facts, discovered a lot of hidden truths and secrets, and endured the emotional roller coaster and consequences that result from undergoing IVF.

This book is not a novel or a collection of personal reflections. As stated in the preface, my intention is to provide factual data that women and couples can learn from and use. As far as I know, other books about infertility do not contain details on the latest IVF trends and facts, along with experiences from the patient's perspective. In addition, although this book contains a lot of medical information, it is not a medical textbook or an instructional guide; however, it does offer firsthand advice and experiential guidance. Throughout the book, I use medical terms and jargon from IVF industry. The appendix contains explanations of these terms, as well as lists of useful Internet links, resources, books, etc.

It is not my intention to seek to replace doctors and other professionals involved in ART. They have all the expertise, education, and experience required to treat ART patients. As explained in the preface, my intention is merely to share the experiences I gained as a fertility patient, in order to help others experiencing fertility problems, including those already going through IVF. I believe less in miracles and more in science, and throughout the book I offer as many facts and details about my journey through IVF as I possibly can, along with my opinions and an honest account of my story. To that end, this book reflects my opinion and my point of view on every aspect of my IVF struggle. Some facts and sequencing related to my fertility protocols, as well as my interpretations, descriptions, wording, explanations, opinions, etc., regarding the laboratory results, scientific terms, approaches and methods, doctors' explanations, recommendations, advice, etc., may not necessarily be correct, as a result of lack of evidence, lack of proper understanding, and/or inaccurate remembering on my part; in addition, the flow of the story may not exactly correspond to the actual sequence of events. All content in this book reflects only my own understanding, intuition, feelings, and recollections, based on explanations by professionals, information from the Internet and different books, as well as from my own instincts. No doctor, nurse, or other staff involved in my husband's and my treatments has any responsibility for my interpretation and understanding of the results, methods, procedures, protocols, or any other information and activities involved while I was undergoing fertility treatments. Also, I do not take responsibility for, and I shall not be liable for, any facts, interpretations, advice, and/or any other information provided in this book. Any medical or nonmedical information and conclusions derived from this book, directly or indirectly, should be checked, confirmed, and/or verified by professionals.

This book does not disclose the real names of any persons, clinics, locations, contacts, websites, or similar Internet links providing information about infertility and IVF in general (except for the list of Internet links, resources, books, etc., provided in the appendix for reference purposes).

* * * * *

This book describes one of the worst-case scenarios in infertility. It is not a story about female infertility or male infertility; it is a story about the combined male and female fertility conditions that influence a couple's infertility. In my husband's and my case, the initial diagnosis was male infertility; however, over time, we had to deal with more-significant issues, including female age factor, poor ovarian reserve, and low responding factor, combined with the male infertility. Our case can also fall under the category of secondary infertility, because, luckily, during the first phase of IVF, we experienced the birth of a healthy baby, our daughter.

Part I of this book is a chronicle of my experiences as an IVF patient. In this section, I share medical information, facts, and valuable experience gained during IVF treatments. It is divided in four chapters describing four stages of patients' journey through IVF: The Hopeful Beginning, Reality Checks on IVF, Pushing the Limits of IVF and Hardships of IVF Closure. In order to not deprive those who wish to understand the science from having the detailed descriptions of IVF protocols, but at the same time to not confuse and overload those not interested in that level of detail, I include in the appendix tables and lists that summarize the IVF treatments/protocols in chronological order, corresponding to the stages of my infertility battle. These tables and lists include summaries of the ART procedures we underwent, medical information about the timing and type of the treatments/protocols, medications and doses prescribed in the protocols, and descriptions of the protocol outcomes.

This book also describes the emotional impact of IVF, including its impact on marriage and relationships. I describe my own turmoil when I decided to end IVF (IVF closure) after many years of living in the "IVF bubble." Facing the cruel reality of failing to conceive more children through IVF caused much heartache and emotional stress, leading to turbulent times in my marriage (my husband was ready to leave me because of our inability to have a big family, a dream we'd always shared), and I share these experiences as candidly as I share the medical ones.

In some places, it may appear that I am repeating information, and often I am. Some things are just too significant to ignore or push aside, so if I repeat myself—it is only to emphasize and reemphasize how crucial it is to be a proactive and informed patient.

Part II of this book offers valuable advice, recommendations, and tools. Again, resources, references, and terminology all are provided in the appendix.

My experiences are unique, yet typical. My journey through the world of IVF can show others how to be proactive, how to avoid the same mistakes I made. It can also warn of some risks that I hadn't anticipated, thereby offering ways for women and couples to protect themselves, to make more-informed choices, to take the correct steps and make the best decisions at the appropriate time—and even more important, to not take the wrong steps or do things at the wrong time. Time management is extremely important, both short-term (i.e., during the treatments) and long-term (i.e., after treatments and ongoing). In fact, long-term time management is even more important than short-term. My most important message to all of you reading this, and to other women everywhere, is simply this: don't wait—make the most of your natural biological reproductive abilities as soon as possible . . . it's easier for all of us when we are younger. Almost as important as managing time is managing money and organizing, and I offer some practical ideas and tips on how to organize IVF, how to apply some principles of project management and how to save money for IVF.

I had another intention in writing this book: I wanted to raise awareness about female fertility and reproductivity potential. I came to regret how much I did not know and how misinformed I was, mostly because of the media, but also because of misinformation from some professionals. I paid a high price for what I did not know, and for the incorrect perceptions I believed. For example, I knew that after a certain age it was more difficult for a woman to conceive, but my understanding was that the "risky" age started in the early to mid forties. I was definitely not planning to have kids that late, and so I never thought that I would fall into the high-risk category. I always had absolutely regular periods, never had any health problems that might have indicated a risk of infertility, and didn't have any genetic predispositions for infertility (my two grandmothers each had four children, and my mother and sister each had two children, and none of the women in my family had problems conceiving). In my mind, to conceive and become pregnant in my mid or late thirties would not involve any risk. However, I was married to an infertile man, and after a few years of undergoing IVF because of male infertility, I had aged, and I consequently lost my reproductivity potential. My experience was not an atypical one. And there is a new generation of women who, similar to my generation, will be misinformed and misled by the media about the "unlimited" possibilities and choices women will have if they plan to have children later in life. Again, a big motivator for writing this book was to help other women avoid believing misinformation and misconceptions, by providing useful information and sharing my firsthand experience.

In today's Western world, one in six couples faces fertility problems, and that number will likely increase in the future. Unfortunately, my husband's and my story could become reality for millions of couples in the world. Prolonged education, economic factors, recession, unemployment, and the general tendency in the West for young people to establish their careers and status prior to starting a family, all may influence an increase in infertility. This is why it is so important to raise awareness about the real capabilities and limitations of IVF. Consider how many people currently suffering with lung cancer might be healthy if only they would have truly understood all the risks associated with smoking before they lit their first cigarette. Of course, infertility is not the same as cancer, and IVF is not the same as smoking, but people tend to make better choices when they have accurate, honest information. Helping women and couples find accurate, honest information about IVF is one of the most important intentions of this book.

Let me reemphasize my intention of raising awareness about ART methods in general, and about the capabilities, limitations, and success rates of IVF procedures. This book reveals some of IVF's "hidden truths," which I discovered while undergoing various treatments; most of these truths contradict the misinformation and misinterpretations promulgated by the media. I have a very traditional approach and attitude now, after seven years of undergoing IVF treatments, learning so much information, and gathering so many facts; going through the protocols and treatments showed me that the success of IVF is very limited and widely misinterpreted. In my opinion, the media exaggerates the success of IVF procedures. In addition, the media provides insufficient and often false information, producing a counteraction of misleading women and causing much more infertility in general. Many women are convinced that IVF can create miracles, and thus, many of them believe that delaying motherhood is no longer associated with the risk of staying childless, as it used to be before IVF was an option. I have met and know of women in their early forties, and even in their late forties, who visited, or planned to visit, a fertility clinic for the first time, believing that they could still easily have a biological baby through IVF. And I know women who are in their mid and late forties still using contraception. No one can blame these women for their misconceptions, as the media features many stories about women having babies, even twins, when in their midforties and shocking stories about women being pregnant in their fifties and even sixties. All this leads to many women misinterpreting the information. They do not worry about their decisions to delay motherhood, because the media misleads them by displaying "living proof" of successful IVF. As a result, women believe that when they are ready to have a baby, if they cannot conceive naturally, they can simply undergo fertility treatment, as long as they can afford to pay for it. In other words, the media gives the impression that in the wonderful modern world we live in, science has overcome the limitations of the female biological clock. The many women who believe that are likely to pay the high price of going through IVF and still remaining childless—and it isn't merely a financial price but much more a physical and emotional.

Perhaps mothers who belong to baby boomers generation or Generation X (born from the early 1960s to the early 1980s) will want to give this book to their daughters who belong to the Generation Y (millennial generation, born from the early 1980s to the mid 1990s) or Generation Z (today's teens and children born from mid 1990s to 2010). Mothers have a responsibility to educate their daughters about female biological clock and to warn them not to delay their own motherhood. The problem nowadays is that mothers are also misinformed and under a wrong impression that female biological clock was something that existed in their time, but does not or will not exist in their daughters time. Mothers should understand the reality and alert their daughters; otherwise, many successive generations of women in this world will undergo IVF (and even if they do, many will still stay childless). This book provides a real-life example and experiential advice that supports the old-fashioned, traditional approach to fertility and female biological clock, which is still well established in some societies, mostly in third world countries, but no longer in most of Western civilization. I hope that this book will reach some younger women and help them prevent a fertility disaster, which is where the generation of younger women may find themselves if they decide to delay motherhood, influenced by the media and general false information about ART. The advices that I am going to give to my daughter is summarized in the chapter: Epilogue/Letter to my Daughter.

This book also addresses a point greatly overlooked in the IVF industry and in the Western media in general: that in most of the world's cultures, the main purpose of marriage is family; that raising children is where most men and women find their greatest and most important purpose in life. There are many prejudices associated with families and children, one of which is that men do not have a great desire to have children and that the initiative for having kids almost always comes from women. I would agree that the initiative more often does come from women, and usually it arises earlier in women than men because women are more aware of their biological clock (at least to some extent). However, men often want kids just as much as women do, but men can more easily delay having children, as they do not risk remaining childless because of age. Men often delay having kids if they are not financially capable of supporting a family, because in many societies men are under pressure to be the only "breadwinners" for the future family. And it is not unusual that men want to have a lot of kids in order to establish themselves as more "manly" and as better providers, and also to appear to have a higher social status and greater power, providing them with more help in the family business, especially in very traditional societies. In many societies, similar to the one that I came from, it would be no surprise for a man to leave a woman who wasn't able to "produce" kids for him. Today's IVF industry does not address this risk that may arise through unsuccessful ART treatments, and there is a lack of counseling and protection for women in such cases.

This book seeks to address all of what I have outlined above, and I hope it achieves my goal of helping to inform women and couples. I also wish to apologize to all women undergoing IVF if my mourning over my fate, despite the fact that I had a child through IVF, hurts or offends them. I apologize to all women who had to decide to choose alternative paths, such as donor eggs, surrogacy, adoption, or any other method. I apologize to all one-child families for any unfavorable words about families with one child, for lamenting about the fate of the "only child," and for my conviction that such children might be a greatly handicapped by having no siblings, not only during the childhood but also throughout their whole lifetime. My intention was never to upset or hurt anyone, only to help others, mostly women and couples coping with infertility and undergoing IVF, by sharing my story, my experiences, and the lessons I learned. My greatest hope is that reading this book leads to positive outcomes for as many women and couples as possible!

PART I

SEVEN YEARS
OF IVF TREATMENTS

Success is the ability to go from one failure to another with no loss of enthusiasm.

—Winston Churchill

1

THE HOPEFUL BEGINNING

Our Infertility Problem (Diagnosis)

Shortly after my husband and I got married, we immigrated to North America. We came from the former Soviet Union. Prior to coming to North America, despite the fact that we were highly educated and already in our early thirties, we struggled with unemployment, and we could not even afford to live without financial help from our parents. This led to overall dissatisfaction with life, and consequently, we delayed starting a family. After arriving in North America, it didn't take us long to establish some level of financial stability and job security, and we soon adjusted to our new home. Once my husband and I both had full-time jobs, we immediately started plans for a family.

Some tests were done before we immigrated to North America and had revealed that my husband had a very low sperm count (under four million), of which more than 60 percent was deviated, mortal, or immobile (also referred to as "low motility"). His diagnosis was olygostenospermia toward necrospermia. For that reason we decided to repeat tests immediately when we started plans for family. His doctor said that his sperm count was almost zero and that with his count I could not get pregnant without IVF/ICSI. And doctor told us that there is no way to increase his sperm count. My husband went for the second opinion, where he heard similar explanation. Doctors could not confirm the reason for this; they just asked if there had ever been an infertility diagnosis in the family. Interestingly, his sister was married for ten years, and she and her husband struggled with infertility. She had her child through IVF, when she was close to forty. However, I never thought that his sister's infertility could have been in any way connected to my husband's infertility, as I was convinced that female and male fertility came from different organs and thus had different origins. It never occurred to me that it didn't matter that they were of different genders, it could have still happened. The doctors suspected that there was some genetic disorder in the family that affected their fertility potential, regardless of the fact that my husband and his sister were of different genders. Also, it could have been that in the 1970s they were both given some vaccine that negatively affected fertility, as some resources on the Internet indicate that people who received the whooping cough (pertussis) vaccine when there were kids during the '70s might develop problems with infertility in adulthood.

For some time that we knew my husband's diagnosis, we didn't take it too seriously because we were not aware of how severe it was. But the severity of my husband's diagnosis—that he probably could not have kids naturally—was not ever explained to him, or to us, by any doctor until the time when we seriously started with plans for family.

However, while going through numerous IVF treatments there arose the ironic situation that the male factor was the diagnosis only in the first two treatments, when I was age thirty-six to thirty-nine. When my age was thirty-nine to forty-three, there was just a tiny note in my file about undergoing the IVF with mandatory ICSI (intracytoplasmic sperm injection), because of the male factor, but my age was written in capital letters, along with my diagnosis as a "low responder." The diagnosis was even worse from my forty-first birthday onward, when I started having elevated follicle stimulating hormone (FSH) levels.

IVF/ICSI Protocols in Clinic A

Once we became fully aware of my husband's infertility, we acted immediately, deciding that it was urgent for us to undergo IVF, as doctors explained to us that IVF was our only option, given my husband's diagnosis. At least that was an extremely smart decision, as we had not wasted time trying to conceive naturally for an unreasonably prolonged period, or trying less-invasive ART methods, before enrolling in IVF. We did not want to try holistic approaches and methods, we did not want to rely on nutritionists, acupuncturists, psychics, horoscope readers, sects, spiritual leaders, or anything like that. We understood that our problem was very serious and that it could be treated only with IVF.

We decided to go to the one of the first and most reputable IVF clinics in town. Throughout this book, I will call this first clinic for ART Clinic A.

I will never forget the moment when I stepped into Clinic A for the first time. I was disappointed, and I almost thought that I was in the wrong place when I arrived in the small waiting room, with the tiny reception desk in the corner, similar to the waiting room in our family doctor's office. At that time, I had the perception that a fertility clinic would be very fancy, with a superb interior, and a clean and huge space, probably because I believed that most of the patients were wealthy and/or celebrities. Or perhaps it was because I still had not fully accommodated to North American medical offices, which are basically not much different from lawyers' or accountants' offices. In my home country, doctors worked only in huge hospitals, or other large medical buildings, with huge corridors, huge waiting rooms, huge labs, and huge operating rooms. In our home country, all medical institutions were very spacious, even monumental in size.

However, my other impression of the clinic mattered much more. I couldn't believe the attitude of the clinic staff: they acted as if they were working in a funeral home rather than a fertility clinic. The atmosphere in the waiting room was silent and cold, and when the nurse finally called my name, she met me in her office without a smile, declaring sternly and quickly what I was supposed to do, as if I had come there to invest in the stock market, not in my ovaries. Somehow I had the expectation that I would be treated with compassion and special care, as a woman with the big problem of not being able to conceive naturally. Instead, most of the time and with the most of the clinic staff, I felt like "just another patient."

When we were accepted as first-time IVF patients at Clinic A, I had to undergo laparoscopy under total anesthesia. Laparoscopy did not reveal anything wrong with my uterus, ovaries, or fallopian tubes, and so the doctors concluded that I was fertile. They performed tests on my husband, which confirmed that his diagnosis had been correct and his situation was very bad, showing no more than two million sperm. Based on this information, the doctors recommended IVF long Lupron protocol, followed by ICSI. The doctors explained that in our case, with the low sperm count and motility, they would not recommend traditional IVF, where fertilization occurs in a "petri dish," with the sperm and egg incubated together with the ratio of about 75,000:1; instead, they recommended the ICSI method, where a single sperm is injected directly into one egg. After that, the fertilized egg is passed to a special growth medium and left for about forty-eight hours, or until the egg consists of few cells, at which point it is called an embryo. And then, usually on the third day (seventy-two hours after the egg retrieval), an embryo transfer is performed. The quality of embryos is determined by having it symmetrically divided into an even number of cells. If an embryo has eight cells on the third day after the retrieval, it is a good indication that it may implant and develop.

They then explained the long Lupron protocol to us in detail. I had to self-inject Lupron every day, starting from about two weeks before I expected my period (better for a few days more than a few days less, they told me). Once I got my period, I was supposed to call the clinic and come every day for blood work and every few days for an ultrasound. Starting from day three of the cycle, I was supposed to inject the prescribed amount of Gonal-F, in addition to continuing the injections of Lupron. I was supposed to call the clinic every day, a few hours after the blood work was done, when clinic already had results of my hormonal levels, and get my prescription for the hormonal injections I needed at night. When doctor determined the time for retrieval of eggs, I was supposed to inject, at the very precise time, 36 hours before the time of egg retrieval, the hormone known as human chorionic gonadotropin (hCG), which would trigger ovulation, as the rest of the protocol intentionally suppressed my ovulation. And finally, doctor will tell me the exact time to arrive at the clinic for my follicles to be retrieved. After retrieval, eggs will be stored in media and ICSI performed with my husband's "best" selected sperm. Eggs will be stored in media in the lab to develop and two days after the retrieval they shall be divided in minimum four cells, eight would be optimal and at that time they will be called embryos. Doctor will perform embryo transfer and after the transfer I will be putting Prometrium vaginal suppositories daily, until the pregnancy test, which will follow in two weeks time. (As explained in the introduction, details about my IVF protocols are summarized in the tables in the Appendix. A more detailed explanation of the long Lupron protocol and medications used in the protocol can be found in the Appendix also, under the List of Terms.)

I was excited to do my first IVF. I had injected the Lupron daily for about two weeks prior to the first day of my period, and on the third day of my cycle, I started injecting 250 units of Gonal-F, along with the Lupron. However, in the very first days of monitoring my cycle, my estradiol level went up, and the clinic canceled the treatment. They discovered that I had an ovarian cyst, and they gave me Minovral, a contraceptive pill. After that, for the first time since I'd started menstruating, I didn't have a period for more than thirty days. The doctors then prescribed Provera, a pill to induce my period. At the time, I was told that once my hormones normalized, I could start IVF protocols again.

Two months later, I went through the one, almost "by the book" long Lupron protocol. I ended up with four follicles ready for retrieval. (Details about this IVF protocol are summarized in the Table 1 in the Appendix, under the 2nd protocol.) Before the final decision for retrieval of my follicles was supposed to be made, by my husband and me, the main nurse called me in her office. She declared that the doctors strongly recommended that I cancel the treatment at that point, as there was a low number of follicles to be retrieved. She continued that statistics were not on my side; with just four follicles and hopefully four eggs retrieved out of them, the probability of a successfully implanted an embryo would have been very low. That moment in the IVF protocol was not only the milestone for the decision of whether it would be worth it for the patient to have a mini surgery for egg retrieval under general anesthesia (as at that time egg retrievals were still done under general anesthesia), but also a financial milestone, because at that point, prior to retrieval of eggs and ICSI fertilization of eggs, expense for the protocol was about four times less than the total expense for the completed protocol.

I was still sitting in the office of the main nurse, and she was impatiently waiting for me to sign the paper, either to accept proceeding with the protocol or to cancel the whole protocol at that point, prior to retrieval. I asked her if I could call my husband to discuss with him what the doctors suggested so that we could make the final decision together. My husband's opinion was that we should follow the doctors' recommendations. I explained to him that there was no guarantee that with only four follicles we wouldn't end up with a baby and that my feeling was that clinic didn't want to take responsibility for exposing us to the expenses, with the lower probability of a positive outcome. I told him that I was ready and that without a doubt I wanted to proceed with the retrieval.

The scary fact is that if I didn't make that decision that day (in fact, I made the decision within approximately fifteen minutes of the nurse's alerting me of the situation and without my husband even agreeing to it), we would have ended up without our only child, as she was born as a result of that protocol! Whenever I think about the moment when I made that decision, I start to shake, and my heart beats faster. What if I had made a different decision? What if I had blindly followed the doctors' recommendations? Our one and only child would have been lost forever in the laboratory fluids. God alone knows for sure, but in all likelihood, we never would have had any children.

Two weeks later, when I was about to hear the results of my pregnancy test, I took off from work and drove to the beach. I walked on the beach and tried to relax. And then I finally got the courage to call the clinic to ask for the result of the pregnancy test. Positive! I couldn't believe it! I was expecting! I had prepared for a long battle to conceive a child, and it happened as a result of the first attempt! I didn't know then that a long battle would later become my destiny. If I only knew then that I would never again hear the same answer! If I only knew! But that is what life is about: unpredictability and challenge.

Thinking about this happy scary story, when just one quick decision could have left us without our child and even childless, I also feel overwhelming happiness and power, as we beat fate at least once. Through the coming years of struggling with IVF, that feeling of happiness and power gave me strength and faith that I might again have a child, despite all the scientific facts, success rates, and statistics. Later, during many more years of unsuccessful IVF/ICSI protocols in the aim to have more children, I wanted to copy that very first protocol. I hoped that the same combination of protocol preparation—prescription for hormonal injections, my body's response, and even the same time of year—might lead to pregnancy, just as it had that very first time. Afterward, there were many more similar long Lupron protocols, just with the higher doses of Gonal-F. However, the Provera pill prescribed to induce my period was never repeated in any other protocol. I still believe that taking the Provera pill before starting the regular long Lupron protocol could have played a key role in getting me pregnant, as that was the only difference between the one successful long Lupron protocols and all the unsuccessful ones—apart from the fact that in future protocols, my youngest age was already thirty-nine.

I was thirty-nine, and my baby was already one and a half years old; I stopped breast-feeding her and was eager to start with IVF again. I could not wait to go back to Clinic A.

After pregnancy and childbirth, I underwent three long Lupron protocols. At that time, because of my age and suspected low-responder status, I was given a higher dose of Gonal-F. In the first protocol after pregnancy, doctors prescribed 375 units of Gonal-F; in the second protocol, 450; and in the third, 500. None of the protocols worked. These three IVF/ICSI treatments were all done within twelve months. As I continued with treatment after treatment, doctors concluded that my chances were slim. At that time, I was still a sole beginner, believing that we would have a baby without any problem, because the only problem, as I was convinced at that time, was a male factor, which was to be overcome with application of ICSI. My husband and I were not investigating and researching IVF beyond the information we were given in the clinic. We enjoyed being babysat by the clinic and clinic staff. Whatever they suggested and told us, we didn't question; but it didn't ever occur to us that anything could be done differently. We thought that we should not interfere with professionals who, with all their knowledge, education, expertise, professionalism, and experience, knew exactly what they were doing. I still do not question the expertise of any fertility doctor that I met through my struggle for a baby; however, now I believe that we should have been better informed about the IVF, in order to make proper decisions in an appropriate time frame, and I also believe that at certain points in the early protocols, we should have taken the lead in the IVF process, as we did during the later years of IVF.

After three unsuccessful long Lupron protocols, I finally learned that I was a low responder and that I had elevated FSH levels, which was all not that unexpected for my age. But I still could not believe that it would be absolutely impossible for me to have another baby, as I was always healthy and never had problems with my period or ovulation; I did not have cysts, or endometriosis or any other indication of infertility. At each protocol, my response was good, except for the fact that I never generated more than two to three eggs. The rest was as expected: my estradiol levels were rising, my follicles were growing, eggs were retrieved, and my husband's sperm was injected. Then the embryos grew to a few cells, were transferred and monitored, but I never ended up getting pregnant. (Details about these IVF protocols are summarized in the Table 1 in the Appendix.)

No matter my first impressions, Clinic A for the few years remained a sacred and loving place for me. After the little life started in one tiny tube in the laboratory of Clinic A, that clinic became my second home and my temple. And I kept on going to the same clinic after my child was born, still hoping for a second and third child. And my hope still lived, all the while I waited for hours in the waiting room, when having blood work or egg retrievals, and when resting after embryo transfers. My hope of having more kids, while I was going to Clinic A, was still very much alive. Even today, after so many years, when I pass by Clinic A, I start crying, not for the unborn babies but for the baby I was lucky enough to get, almost by an accident.

Side Effects of Hormonal IVF Protocols

The common belief, at least in fertility clinics, is that there is no known harm or extra risk for women undergoing fertility treatments. Although I didn't experience any serious health problems after the many IVF/ICSI protocols that I went through, I am not convinced that one day in the future, a woman who underwent several IVFs could not face ovarian or breast cancer or some other illness. My belief is that the data on female IVF patients is still insufficient for researchers to draw meaningful scientific conclusions as to the possible consequences that different ART treatments may have on women's health. The data that exists does not reflect a significant number of women studied over a sufficient length of time, in my opinion.

During the IVF treatments, when I was usually undergoing aggressive hormonal stimulation, I did not feel entirely well, and I experienced the common side effects of being "pumped" hormonally. The following is a list of the physical, mental, and emotional conditions/symptoms that I experienced while on IVF treatments:

- fear of total anesthesia
- tiredness, dizziness, inability to concentrate
- nervousness, hypersensitivity, mood swings, grumpiness
- being superstitious
- increased appetite before, during, and after the protocol; weight gain
- feeling bloated
- abdominal pain and cramps
- feeling pregnant
- delayed and different-than-usual periods
- ovarian cysts
- variations in libido; prolonged sexual abstention
- menopause symptoms

Let me give some details about each of the conditions/symptoms listed above.

Fear of Total Anesthesia

During the first few years of undergoing IVF, egg retrievals were still done under total anesthesia. The first time I went under this anesthesia, I was afraid that I would never wake up again. But over time, after undergoing total anesthesia several times, I started thinking about it as a mysterious moment when I would suddenly get to sleep and disappear, and then wake up with the future baby beginning its life. Regardless of what these thoughts and fears of general anesthesia might have been, they were not strong enough to discourage me from having more protocols to achieve a pregnancy.

Tiredness, Dizziness, Inability to Concentrate

Throughout the IVF protocols I still went regularly to my full-time job. I continuously felt very tired and very sleepy, even as early as around noon, and I often wished to take a nap in the middle of the day, which was impossible. I was not always able to concentrate, and I occasionally experienced memory problems. I also felt dizzy quite often, especially while in the car and on elevators.

Hypersensitivity, Mood Swings, Nervousness, Grumpiness

During the treatments I was hypersensitive and often overreacted. I screamed at my husband for not putting his dirty socks in the laundry bag, and I cried in the supermarket when I saw the image of a happy baby's face on a package of diapers. During the early days of a protocol, it was not unusual for me to become angry without too much reason, swear nervously, or throw stuff around.

Being Superstitious

Throughout most of the time that I underwent IVF, I found myself being superstitious. I constantly saw "signs" of success or failure of the treatment. I would open the calendar to the exact month when the baby from that protocol could possibly be born, or I would see ten pregnant women on the day of an embryo transfer. There was also a time when I believed that the more contact I had with pregnant women, the more likely I was to get pregnant.

Increased Appetite before, during, and after the Protocol; Weight Gain

During the protocols, I felt hungry all the time, and I had to eat something almost every hour. Normally I could endure feeling hungry for a long time if necessary, and I usually did not have uncontrolled cravings for food. My weight and figure prior to IVF were not perfect, but if I wanted to have close-to-perfect body weight, I didn't have to lose more than seven to ten pounds. However, while undergoing IVF, I was continually carried about twenty-two pounds of extra weight, and I had a very big belly, especially during the time of treatments. This went on for several years.

Feeling Bloated

During the protocols, I always felt like a big balloon, more and more bloated with each passing day.

Abdominal Pain and Cramps

In the last days of each protocol, when the follicles grew large, I usually felt abdominal pain and cramps. After the egg retrieval, I felt even more severe pain and cramps.

Feeling Pregnant

During some treatments, especially after embryo transfers, I would feel and recognize definite signs of being pregnant, such as pain in my abdomen, an uncomfortable feeling in my uterus, fatigue, breast enlargement, dizziness, change in appetite, increased libido, etc.

These signs of pregnancy typically appeared in order and repeated themselves in a similar manner after the IVF treatments:

Third day after embryo transfer: feeling good, relaxed, and calm

Fourth day after transfer: cramps in my lower belly and the feeling that my period would soon arrive

Nights between fourth, fifth, and sixth day: insomnia

Fifth day: breasts firmer and slightly enlarged

Sixth day: very strong feeling that I was actually pregnant, although at the same time I felt that my period was about to start

Seventh day: very hungry; craving salty food

Eighth day: very sleepy in the middle of the day; sensitive and emotional (when I saw a mother with a baby, I would start to cry); strong sweat odor

Ninth day: difficulty concentrating; memory problems (trouble remembering computer passwords, etc.)

Delayed and Different-than-Usual Periods

I sometimes waited for my period for up to fifty days, and I was concerned that the IVF treatments might negatively impact my natural reproductivity and fertility potential, and even that I might be having early menopause symptoms. Also, during the time between treatments, I occasionally experienced menstrual bleeding that was greater or less than usual, as well as periods that were longer or shorter than usual.

Ovarian Cysts

My treatments had to be canceled because of ovarian cysts quite a few times. Once, in the middle of the night, I experienced terrible pain in my ovary, which was comparable only to contractions. I went to the emergency room, and the doctor told me that it was probably a ruptured cyst.

Variations in Libido; Prolonged Sexual Abstention

I experienced higher—and lower-than-usual sex drive, and these variations in my libido were likely caused by the hormonal therapy. Also, my husband's and my intimate life was very much affected because, while undergoing IVF treatments, we had to go through prolonged abstention periods, for as long as six weeks at times.

Menopause Symptoms

During the Depo Lupron protocol, I experienced severe headaches and hot flashes (it is described in detail in the chapter about menopause induction protocol). I worried that I was going through early menopause.

Learning That I Was a Low (Poor) Responder

It is my understanding that the objective of IVF protocols for every woman, regardless of the clinic or the type of protocol, is to have the minimum number of IVF treatments, with the maximum number of eggs, resulting in a healthy baby (or babies). Unfortunately, however, many women are low responders, just like I am. A *low responder* is defined as a woman who does not respond well to hormonal stimulation designed to produce multiple eggs in one cycle. Usually the cutoff number of follicles (which may or not contain the egg) that defines a low responder is four to five. However, according to some definitions, a low responder is also a woman whose peak estradiol level under hormonal stimulation is up to 500. (This refers to the woman's estradiol level just before the injection that triggers ovulation and prior to egg retrieval.) I was never in that category, as my peak estradiol levels were between 3,000 and 4,000 during my thirties and between 2,000 and 3,500 up until age forty-three. As I understand it, the low responder factor is in direct proportion to the woman's age and reproductive reserve.

In my case, during the first complete protocol when I received a relatively low dose of Gonal-F (250 units), I was probably already a low responder, even at the age of thirty-seven. I had only four eggs retrieved and two embryos transferred, resulting in the birth of my sweet baby. I was entirely overwhelmed with happiness upon becoming the mother of a healthy baby through IVF. I didn't ask the doctors for more information about our fertility case, and I had a lack of understanding of IVF in general, and of the capabilities and limitations of fertility treatments. Convinced that if it worked for us on the very first attempt, there would be no problems with future IVF protocols, I saw no reason to ask any questions. I simply believed we would be able to have as many babies as we wanted. At that time, the doctors did not share their concerns that I might be a low responder; we did not learn that until few years later.

I waited a year and a half before returning to Clinic A for the next baby. I was breast-feeding my daughter, and I simply loved that incredible bond with my baby. I had to go back to work when the baby was close to her first birthday, and I did not want to stop breast-feeding, so I even had to pump breast milk while at work. I probably would have decided to prolong breast-feeding if not for the fact that one evening, totally exhausted from the nighttime feedings and working full-time, I just fell out of the breast-feeding chair with the baby in my arms. That was a definite sign for me that the time had come to stop breast-feeding! My regular periods had already started about six months after giving birth to my baby, but the doctors had explained that while breast-feeding, I would not be able to get pregnant.

Thus, the time had come to stop breast-feeding, to regain fertile periods, and to return to the clinic for more babies. Let me reemphasize that at that time I didn't have a clue that I might be a low responder. I was convinced that the only reason we had to go to the clinic was my husband's low sperm count, not my infertility. So, blissfully unaware of the brutal decline of my fertility and reproductivity potential, I began checking my menstrual calendar and calculating dates for possible egg retrieval and embryo transfer, as well as dates for the birth, possible names, and even trying to plan the baby's astrological sign! I had no idea that women who responded well to IVF hormonal stimulation had way more than two to four eggs retrieved; most had more than ten, and some even had more than twenty.

I did not find out that I was a low responder until my fourth IVF protocol. Even now, I don't understand why the doctors didn't explain that fact to me at the beginning, when I first conceived (my daughter). I understand that not every cycle is as fertile as the next, and only with repeated low-responding cycles does it become obvious that a patient is a low-responder, so in my case, after the very first complete protocol under a relatively low dose of hormonal stimulation, my doctors probably could not have been entirely sure that I would be a low responder, especially given that my peak estradiol level was around 4,000. Also, I was initially in IVF just because of my husband's infertility. I was still not too old (thirty-seven), so the doctors probably believed that by exposing me to the better responding cycle and higher doses of gonadotropins, they would be able to retrieve more eggs, and then I could have ended up with twins, or even some embryos to freeze. However, there still was a good possibility that I was a low responder, and I just wish that they would have given me that information.

In my later IVF treatments, it became obvious that I was almost a textbook example of a low responder, as my body rejected any high dose of hormonal stimulation; in addition, no matter the cycle, hormonal dose, or type of stimulation, the maximum number of eggs retrieved was two to three. Some doctors gave me the highest doses of gonadotropins throughout the protocol (up to 600 units); some were limited me to 400 units, believing that my body would just reject higher doses, and I think this was the correct approach. I have since read about the theory that female low responders to IVF hormonal stimulation actually have a lower risk of developing problems as a result of hormonal stimulation, because their bodies reject the additional hormones, staying in tune with the natural hormonal levels, but having a less chances to conceive through IVF.

If, during the very early IVF stage, I had been aware that the doctors might have already suspected that I was a low responder, I would certainly have been more concerned and probably would have decided to try for a second baby as soon as my period returned after giving birth to my daughter. When starting with IVF again, after my daughter was born, I was still convinced that the only problem was my husband's infertility, which was overcome by the ICSI method, and that I was an entirely healthy and fertile woman. That conviction was based not only on the fact that I conceived in my first complete IVF/ICSI attempt, but also on my very regular and healthy gynecological history throughout many years, as well as my not having any indication about my fertility problem or any problematical gynecological diagnosis in my immediate family.

I wish I had known, when I was thirty-seven, that not only I, but almost every woman from the midthirties on, already has a diminished egg reserve, is expected to have a rapid decrease in fertility, and if not already a low responder to the hormonal stimulation introduced with ART, will likely become a low responder in a very short period of time. If I'd known these facts at that time, I would most likely have been under more stress, and I would have rushed to start new protocols immediately after the birth of my child.

Now I understand that once a woman reaches a certain age, usually about thirty-five, the time frame for trying to conceive naturally or with IVF is crucial. I believe that I wasted valuable time because I was not properly informed. I wouldn't have made a more-than-two-year break in IVF treatment following the birth of my child, and then again for almost a year when my husband underwent varicocele surgery, when I was already forty. I wouldn't have wasted that valuable year when I still probably had a better chance to conceive through IVF. There is no guarantee that I would have succeeded, but I would have undergone more IVFs before the age of forty, and I probably would have asked for a second opinion in more clinics sooner in the process; I definitely would have explored other options. Also, with the earlier awareness of being a low responder, I would have most probably decided to undergo natural IVF protocols (described in chapter 3).

The Early IVF Stage and Its Impact on Our Relationship and Marriage

During the early IVF stage, I had a great support from my husband in general. We were both overwhelmed with happiness because of our healthy baby daughter, and we were full of hope for more children. At that time, despite the fact that I had a baby, that I worked full-time, and that I took care of all household duties, I voluntarily accepted the fact that I usually went to the clinics alone, handled the protocol schedules, procedures, and other activities alone, and gave myself injections alone. The fact that I was doing most of the treatment activities alone did not bother me, because at that time I was convinced that my husband and I shared responsibilities on a fair and correct basis. I respected the fact that my husband had to work hard to build a successful career; he had to continue working long hours and sometimes even over the weekends, in order to be a "money machine" for the enormously expensive fertility treatments. But what bothered me was that he was often too busy to even call me or e-mail at the time of some treatment milestones, such as the arrival of important results and the doctors' instructions and opinions on the anticipated success of each protocol. Usually, he would even forget to ask me about the number of follicles and eggs retrieved, the most important information during the whole protocol other the pregnancy test! During the IVF protocols, as I've already explained, I had many unpleasant side effects and did not always feel well. My husband almost never called me at work to check on how I was feeling. Possibly that was because of my tendency not to complain, even when I didn't feel well (which would happen often during aggressive hormone treatments). I simply assumed that he felt empathy and concern, even if he didn't express it and that he was too busy at work to be able to babysit me.

Occasionally, we had unpleasant arguments. Instead of acknowledging and endorsing me for how much physical and spiritual strength and energy I needed to muster in order to go through these difficulties and yet maintain normal day-to-day activities, including a full-time career, caring for our child, and all my other household duties, he took it all for granted. He also accused me of spending too much money and laid the blame on for some mutual past decisions, even accusing me of deciding to delay having children. That sometimes led me to feel completely abandoned by him. The heavy hormone treatments probably intensified this feeling. My feelings of loneliness and anger would sometimes lead to self-pity, and even to more arguments with my husband: I would cry, overreact, and become overly sensitive (again, the hormones and steroids used in treatment probably exacerbated this).

On the other hand, my husband was always with me when it was most important, such as for the egg retrievals and embryo transfers. At the very beginning of our struggle, when I was in hospital for the laparoscopy, we were both scared; it was the first surgery under general anesthesia that I had ever experienced. The last thing I remember before I fell asleep was my husband waving to me and crying.

Most of the time, my husband and I were not in the same state of mind. When I was down, he would be in good spirits and full of hope, saying, "So what? We'll go for another trial!" When he was losing hope, I was the one to bring his spirits up. That helped us to overcome depression sooner and to psychologically endure the treatments. Our frustration definitely cannot be compared to the couple who tried several times without succeeding. I had a baby from my first-ever complete IVF treatment, and I never let me disappointments or frustrations overshadow my gratitude for my daughter, or my joy in motherhood. For us, the nightmare didn't start at the beginning of the IVF journey, or even at the beginning of IVF for the second child, but sometime in the middle and final stages.

We kept our struggle for another baby a secret for a long time. The main reason was that we didn't want our child and future children to feel different and strange. Also, we didn't like the idea of strangers knowing and discussing our problem or feeling sorry for us. But the fact that my husband and I, individually and as a couple, lived for years in the "IVF bubble", without communicating about IVF, analyzing the situation, or just simply sharing our IVF experiences with anyone, backfired at the end of the process.

2

REALITY CHECKS ON IVF

Leaving Clinic A; Varicocele Surgery and Trying IUI

After three ICSI long Lupron/Gonal-F protocols in an attempt to have a second child through IVF in Clinic A, we decided to follow the advice to take a minimum six-month break, in order for my hormonal system to recover, relax, and return to normal. At that same time, my husband underwent varicocele surgery. He was the one who insisted undergoing this surgery, and he showed great regret for not having done it when he was younger, before we even started with IVF. Maybe he felt guilty that I had to go through all the hormonal stimulation and treatments and that my life was completely absorbed by IVF, all because of his infertility, while his only "job" was to produce sperm for the egg insemination through ICSI, to occasionally drive me to the clinic, and to accompany me on days of egg retrieval and embryo transfer. In any event, he hoped that his condition might improve after the surgery, but unfortunately, that didn't happen. After the varicocele surgery it was expected that there would be a decrease in sperm count for a few months, but that afterward there would be possible improvement. In his case, there was never any improvement. The removal of the blood veins, which the doctor suspected was warming the sperm and negatively affecting it, didn't seem to make any difference in his spermogram. His surgeon reported that after bilateral varicocelectomy there was a modest improvement in the sperm parameters, but the sperm count was certainly too low for a chance of spontaneous pregnancy. He advised him to use IVF.

During the six-month break in IVF treatments, while we were waiting for spermogram to improve, we did intrauterine insemination (IUI) three times, using a doctor who specialized in IUI. My results did not show any abnormalities, even without stimulation, or with the very low hormonal stimulation, but after the third unsuccessful IUI, the doctor recommended that we should undergo IVF/ICSI protocols. (I later learned that this was by the book, following a third unsuccessful IUI attempt.)

I met a few women who were advised to do IUI while they were in their early thirties, probably because their doctors were not concerned about sending them to IVF immediately, as they were not yet past thirty-five. Some of them told me that they regretted wasting so many years on IUI, and not moving to IVF while they were younger and thus more likely to get pregnant through IVF. One of them was my husband's sister, who could not conceive through IUI (which she tried for several years), and who conceived through her first IVF.

First Rejection in Fertility Clinic

A few months after the varicocele surgery, which unfortunately ended without any improvement in my husband's spermogram, we were ready to start IVF/ICSI treatment again. It became obvious to us that we had to leave Clinic A, where we just kept repeating the same long Lupron protocol without any success. It was only a week before my forty-first birthday when I decided to go for a second opinion, and then I started shopping around for a new clinic.

The doctor that I went to see for a second opinion sounded like a television personality, like she was reading her lines; most probably she was doing exactly that, as precaution to prevent liability. She told me that with my previous history and the recent results showing my elevated FSH, my chances for getting pregnant were very low, and I shouldn't waste any more money; I should consider stopping treatments, she said, and instead spend money on traveling and enjoying life.

I was in a state of shock after hearing this doctor's recommendations. I was totally unprepared for hearing something like that, as I had my child as a result of a successful first attempt with IVF; plus, only three months before, another doctor had accepted me for IUI on a natural cycle! And she delivered this opinion just a few days before I turned forty-one. I felt angry and devastated. I had never felt that desperate in my fertility battle up until that moment.

As soon as I recovered from this newfound despair, I decided to continue with IVF. I realized that I did not have the luxury of taking breaks, taking it easy, going through the same kind of protocols in the same clinic. I felt compelled to organize future fertility protocols very aggressively, with an emphasis on time management. It was an eye-opener that my chances were actually very slim, but I was still convinced that with a hard work I could beat the odds. And the next day, when my shock and disappointment faded away, I decided to do whatever I could to deal with that goddamned FSH.

After some Internet research on FSH, I wasn't convinced that high FSH was a definite sign that I could not have a baby. It was just an indication that I had a diminished number of eggs, which I already knew because of my diagnosis as a "low responder." However, I just needed one good-quality egg, not a dozen. I didn't consider, even for a moment, to accept the advice to stop fertility treatments. I decided to go to the new clinic. I was in a panic and extremely upset.

After investigating the issue of elevated FSH, I reached the conclusion that it might be possible that because my first period occurred after I'd just turned eleven, fertility-wise I was already one or two years older than the average woman, who had her first period at the age of twelve to fourteen. This interpretation of reproductive ability and its connection to the time of the first period is purely my own, and is definitely not scientific and not based on any medical facts.

But right or wrong, that kind of thinking was a wake-up call for me, and I realized that I would have to take some really aggressive steps in a short period of time if I wanted to "catch the last train," and I certainly hoped I would be able to.

Selecting a New Clinic; Introduction of Microflare Protocol with letrozole in Clinic B; Starting with DHEA and Acupuncture

It was very difficult and emotional decision for me to leave Clinic A, where my child was conceived. Clinic A had sentimental value for me, and I felt as if the clinic staff had somehow adopted me (my first impressions of the clinic and staff notwithstanding). In other words, I was a "senior" patient. But I also knew that it was a time to move on. I was not absolutely comfortable with the decision, but I had an urge to explore other opinions and scientific approaches that might give me more options and more chances. I never regretted the decision to change clinics, as doing so opened a new door to more information and education about infertility in general, as well as a better understanding of our infertility diagnosis. And most of all, because that decision led to great hope that in some other clinic, under some different ART protocol, we would succeed.

We chose a clinic that had a good reputation for treating older women, female low responders, and women with elevated FSH levels. (I'll call it Clinic B from hereon.) Clinic B was much fancier than Clinic A; it looked more like a plastic surgery clinic for wealthy patients than an ART clinic. Also, the average age of women in the waiting room was about the same as my age at the time, early forties, which made me feel comfortable and encouraged me that we would succeed. The doctors in the clinic appeared very knowledgeable and open to exploring new approaches and methods in ART. They were willing to think "outside of the box," which wasn't the case with Clinic A, where the doctors were very traditional, and in my case, followed all procedures by the book.

Also, the Clinic B staff all were very nice and kind. In addition, Clinic B's location was convenient for me, which was very important, as I still worked continuously full-time, without any leaves for medical reasons. It was much easier for me to come to Clinic B very early in the morning and still be at work at 9:00 a.m., than to go to Clinic A, which was far away and resulted in my constantly working late to make up time, after not getting to work until 11:00 a.m. on many treatment days.

In Clinic B, over a relatively short period of time, I underwent microflare protocols two times. The microflare protocol was slightly easier and shorter than the long Lupron protocol, because there were no two weeks of injections before my period. It was also easier because I was injecting 150 units of medication in the morning and 150 units in the evening. Microflare started on day two of the cycle, in my case with Suprefact 0.05 and Puregon 300 units. I was also given Femara (letrozole). There was some belief that letrozole could enhance IVF success and pregnancy rates. In the first IVF treatment in Clinic B, I had three eggs retrieved and two grade-1 embryos transferred. In the second protocol doctors decided to change the medication from Puregon to Repronex 300 units. There was only one leading follicle, and for that reason the protocol was canceled. (Details about these two IVF protocols in Clinic B are summarized in the Table 2 in the Appendix, under the 6th and 7th protocol. A more detailed explanation of the microflare protocol and medications used in the protocol can be found in the Appendix also, under the List of Terms.)

Shortly before the second microflare protocol in Clinic B, which was canceled, I started with DHEA. It was a very beginning of introduction of DHEA in fertility treatments and most of the clinics were still reluctant to introduce DHEA preparation before the protocol, as it was still in very experimental phase. (More information about DHEA can be found in Appendix, under the List of Terms.)

I also decided to try to enhance my chances for getting pregnant with the acupuncture. I started shopping around for the acupuncturist. The owner of one acupuncture clinic told me that he had a doctor who had just arrived from China, who almost didn't speak any English, and he admitted that when choosing doctors to work in his clinic, he didn't look for Canadian experience, but Chinese experience. As soon as I heard that, I decided to start acupuncture treatments in that clinic. At the time of the protocol, I was going to the acupuncturist a few times a week. I loved going there. To me, it felt as if the acupuncture clinic actually *was* in China; once I entered the clinic, I felt like I traveled far away, all the way to the Far East. My acupuncturist was a female Chinese doctor who had just recently emigrated from China. She treated me with seriousness and a professional scientific approach, and I was very confident that she was passing on her knowledge of Eastern medicine to enhance my chances to conceive. And I especially liked the traditional

Chinese music she played; it was so relaxing that I almost always slept throughout most of the acupuncture treatment. I was convinced that even if acupuncture did not help me to conceive, that deep relaxing state might help prepare my body to produce a healthy embryo and have a healthy pregnancy.

Introduction of Agonist/Antagonist Protocol in Clinic B; Last Good Protocol

I was still going to Clinic B, waiting for a good cycle without any cysts, so I could start another protocol, which would be the third in Clinic B. I had been taking DHEA for a few months. After the canceled protocol, I had some cysts, and I had to taking contraceptive pills to eliminate them. Finally, after five months of monitoring, everything looked good, and I was ready to start the next protocol. In the meantime I was investigating other clinics and doing cycle monitoring in Clinic C [see Rushing to the New Clinic, later in this chapter].

This time the doctors decided to go with an agonist/antagonist protocol. From day one of my cycle, I took 400 units of Menopur, and from day five, Orgalutran. On day nine, I had an hCG shot, followed by the egg retrieval, and embryo transfer. As usual after the retrieval and transfer I had to take vaginal progesterone suppositories, but this time three times per day and I was taking Doxycycline antibiotic for five days. (Details about this protocol are summarized in the Table 2 in the Appendix, under the 8th protocol. More detailed explanation of the agonist/antagonist protocol and medications used in the protocol can be found in the Appendix also, under the List of Terms.)

In my opinion, that was the best protocol in years, as I ended up having two embryos divided into eight cells and six cells. The reason that I finally had a more natural and better response could be that I was taking DHEA for few months prior to that protocol, or it could be because I was going to an acupuncturist once a week, or it could be that my body had needed a break from hormonal stimulation (I hadn't had a treatment for almost a half a year). Maybe it was a combination of these factors that led to the retrieval of two eggs and the transfer of two grade-1 embryos, divided into eight cells and six cells. And my age at that time was already forty-two and a half! I began to think that I should continue doing the same protocol another few times, including taking DHEA. At that time, researchers were still testing the effects of DHEA, and there were already few a studies published that showed its positive effect on older women and on women with poor ovarian reserve. It appeared that DHEA intake for a few months prior to protocols showed good results to some extent, and that certainly was true in my case.

That is what I think now, but at that time, I was skeptical about the DHEA. We decided to change clinics and go with something absolutely new and promising. But that was when the disaster began.

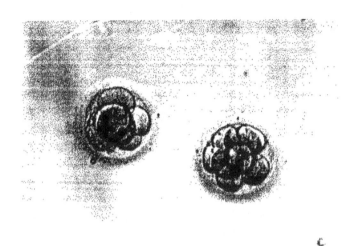

The two grade-1 embryos from agonist/antagonist protocol with Menopur and Orgalutran, and DHEA prior to the protocol. I was forty-two and that was the last good protocol. (Details are provided in Appendix, Table 2, protocol 8)

To Hope or Not to Hope

My frustrations and disappointments with IVF began to grow slowly as my hope for a second child faded. My first disappointment came when I realized that I wouldn't be able to choose a zodiac sign for my future child. Other disappointments soon followed. I realized that my chances for having triplets, or even twins, were very slim. And then I was upset when I realized that the age difference between my children would not be ideal. It hurt when I had to get rid of the few remaining boxes of breast-feeding pads and bags of diapers, all of which were collecting dust while waiting for the second baby. It was painful to acknowledge that I would never need a double stroller for my toddler and newborn, as my daughter was already out of the stroller. I felt sad when I realized that I would never again send a thank-you card to Clinic A, where my daughter was born. And I felt even sadder when I faced the reality that I would not need to send a thank-you card to any clinic ever again.

I understand that doctors, nurses, and clinic staff are probably advised not to give too much false hope to patients. But I wish they would have smiled more or offered more words of encouragement; sometimes they did, but most of the time they didn't. I will never forget the day of my first-ever egg transfer, in Clinic A, when despite all the doctors' skepticism and advice not to proceed, I decided to continue with the transfer of these two little embryos, the only ones I had during that very first protocol. I will never forget the smile on the face of the doctor performing the embryo transfer, followed by his cheerful "good luck!" That meant so much to me. At that moment, I felt so overwhelmed by his smile and kind words, and I realized that despite having a low number of embryos, I should not completely lose hope. Exactly forty-two weeks after that day I gave birth to my only child.

The staff at Clinic B was much kinder, and they seemed more human and emotionally connected to their patients. From their words and behavior, I felt that everything went smoothly and predictably and that I was almost a textbook example of the IVF patient, except for the fact that I was a low responder. At the same clinic, on the day of egg retrieval, I overheard that the woman next to me had twenty-seven eggs retrieved. I couldn't believe it, and when I asked the nurse to confirm, she said that they had retrieved even more! What frustration I felt at that moment! I almost lost all hope, realizing how slim my chances were with a maximum of only three eggs. And I was also puzzled as to why an obviously fertile and young woman would be even undergoing IVF. Finally, after three unsuccessful treatments, the staff informed that I was very aged fertility-wise and that because there was not much hope for me, I should start considering donor eggs. That was a big disappointment for me, as everything seemed fine during the treatments, except that I was a low responder. It felt as if all of a sudden I was considered a premenopausal woman who could not rely on her own eggs anymore. Perhaps this was more my own interpretation than anything said or done by Clinic B staff, but the disappointment overwhelmed me.

At that time, my deepest depression began. Previously, when any one treatment did not succeed, I had always been able to hope that the next treatment would be successful. But with the information that my FSH level was now above 15, I had to face the cruel fact that I had gotten old and was almost no longer fertile—and no artificial method could overcome that. I started to cry more than ever at that point, thinking about how unfair my situation was: my fertility and reproductivity were almost completely gone, and now I had to consider either not having more children, or undergoing IVF treatments with donor eggs. I found myself staring at the faces of pregnant women who looked old, trying to estimate their age, trying desperately to prove to myself that these future mothers might even be older than I was.

At one point, my husband accused me of having lost hope. That really made me angry; it hurt me too. I thought, *Hey, I'm doing all I can! I've always done whatever I could!* For years, I kept trying and trying, with only a three-month break between IVF/ICSI protocols, while at the same time taking steroids (DHEA). Through it all, I stayed very positive. I tried not to worry, to live and eat healthy, to get enough sleep, and to enjoy my time with my child as much as possible. And not only did my husband accuse me of losing hope, he also told me that we would not succeed because I didn't believe in God's support and I didn't pray! He claimed that when his sister, after having suffered ten years of infertility while doing only IUI, started to believe in God and asked for His help, she finally had a child. However, I would like to add that her children were born when she finally decided to go through IVF. I don't mean to sound sarcastic. It's not that I didn't believe in God's help, but I did believe in science, and in our case, I was pretty sure that science, science, and nothing but science, could have helped us.

The time came when I felt that not only was I unlucky, but that I also passed my bad luck on to the clinic and the doctor treating me. Whatever clinics introduced, hoping it would be successful, didn't work for me: changed protocol approach and medications didn't work; acupuncture didn't work; introducing DHEA didn't work. In short, nothing worked well, and much of it even led to more problems and an even worse response than the preceding protocols. I felt, or maybe I just imagined, that even some of the clinic staff thought that I was a bad luck and that it would be better if I disappeared from their clinic, as my case was a constant reminder of the limitations of their science, technology, techniques, and practice; I simply was not adding anything good to their statistics and references.

Now that I have experienced IVF closure (termination of IVF), I cannot say that I miss a day of all those years of living with infertility and going through the IVF protocols. But I greatly miss the days of hoping for a positive outcome, of still believing that my dream of having more children would one day come true.

Falling Apart: How Our Struggle with Infertility Affected Our Relationship, Our Marriage, and Our Child

After a few years of going through IVF, my husband and I became more and more distant. He claimed that our life goals were no longer the same. He kept telling me that his main goal was to leave a legacy: to have more children and leave reasonable wealth for them. My goal was to live and enjoy life, according to him. He insisted that this was so, despite my undergoing IVF for years, all while having a full-time job, being the primary caregiver for our child, and taking care of all the household duties. I felt increasingly alone. I no longer shared my thoughts and concerns with him, and that didn't bother me as before. More and more, I would avoid serious conversations about fertility treatments and our future decisions and steps, especially in the evening, as such conversations would often lead to another sleepless night, at least for me. We still functioned well as partners and parents, though. We were quite organized in our everyday duties and schedules. We were perhaps better partners than ever, but there was a huge emotional gap between us: we hardly communicated with each other anymore, and we were no longer friends. For a long time, we had not gone out on Saturday nights, because there was nothing for us to talk about anymore, except IVF. We stopped laughing, having conversations, and dreaming together. There was no planning, no meaningful discussions, no humor, no leisure time. Up until that time, we had been very social, regularly organizing gatherings and dinner parties. We also went to many theater performances and concerts. But we gradually found ourselves no longer interested in social and cultural life, and we were almost abandoned by our social circle. We were not good company for most people; it wasn't that we told everyone our sad story, but our auras and moods reflected our sadness and frustration. And people don't like to feel overwhelmed by the problems of others; they don't like to be surrounded by dark, negative feelings, or by pessimism and frustration. People like to spend time with happy, cheerful, relaxed friends.

For a long time, my husband was just "technically" my spouse and partner, as he concentrated only on his work. Every day, especially before, during, and after the protocols, I felt more and more betrayed by him, and not only selfishly left alone, when I most needed his support, but also forced to undergo the IVF protocols until "the end of the world," without any concern for my health and well-being. I tried to understand how he felt—that he wanted more kids so badly and that he was not as close to giving up as I was—but I felt like he never thought about how I felt, much less cared. I, on the other hand, was prepared to give up trying to have more kids and to just enjoy my best years with our then four-year-old daughter. He wanted another two kids minimum, but he wasn't even spending enough time with the one child we already had! It appeared to me that he wanted quantity over quality and that he had started to ruin the paradise in which we lived with our daughter from the moment she was born. Or it was only my paradise that I lived in with her through her toddler years and after? It was not as if I didn't have any warning and didn't notice some strange things in my husband's behavior throughout the years of IVF. I did notice, I just didn't pay too much attention to it, and I didn't try to analyze it, because, at that time, I thought that it was part of his depression and unhappiness with our situation, aggravated by too much stress at work. Besides, I was too busy to think about and analyze the situation while working full-time, having a little kid to take care of, doing all the household chores, and undergoing regular IVF treatments for a few years without almost any break between protocols of longer than three months. I was too busy and starting to be stressed with IVF to notice and to be bothered with my husband's lack of love and care for me, because at that time I had much more important things to worry about. Nevertheless, my husband's behavior did show definite signs of not caring for me as he once had, which I later realized were also signs that he had distanced himself from me. He had probably started feeling depressed about the IVF failure even before I had, as it became more and more predictable with each protocol that we would not succeed in our attempt to have more children. As a result, he felt already in conflict with me because it did not seem that we would have more children, which was completely unacceptable to him.

Our infertility struggle not only affected us and our relationship and marriage, it also affected our daughter. God alone knows all the aspects and subconscious impacts that our struggle may have had on her. But there were enough obvious signs of how greatly stressed she was by our infertility frustration. From the age of three, she started to ask for a baby brother or sister. When she was four, we had already told to her that we were seeing doctors who were going to help us to have a baby. She even went with us many times to the clinics. Naturally, she was convinced that a baby comes with the doctor's help.

I realized how much stress we had passed on to our daughter when she was close to her fifth birthday. She started playing her favorite game: she was a female character from a TV show, I was a male character, and we were in love, married, and now she was pregnant. She would put everything from stuffed animals to boxes of tissues under her shirt. Then, I had to play a doctor, asking her if the baby was ready and then giving her a pretend injection in her belly. She would take a deep breath, and then I, as the doctor, would take the baby out of her belly. She liked to play this game over and over, and in the course of ten minutes, she could have as many as five babies! We both enjoyed that game, until one day when my husband overheard us playing. He forbid our playing it again, and I had to agree with him, as it had started to seem morbid for such a young child to be that obsessed with pregnancy. (Not to mention how obsessed I was.)

One day I overheard a conversation between my daughter and one of her friends while the two children were playing in our home. The other girl said, "And because God wanted it, I was born." My daughter very self-confidently replied, "No. Your mother went to see a doctor, and he gave her an injection, and that's how you were born!" The girls were about five years old at the time.

Many times I felt sad watching my daughter playing alone, and even sadder when I thought about her future loneliness for at least the next fifteen to twenty years, when she would still be young, emotional, insecure, vulnerable, and in need of close friends and siblings. I worried about the possible bad choices she might make in the future, with friends, dates, and even a spouse, simply because she might be desperately lonely; I also worried that she might develop egocentric behavior as a result of being an only child, adored and spoiled. Even in early child, having siblings would have helped, not only for playtime and fun activities, but also in her proper development and behavior. It would also have been easier for us to bring her up properly if she'd had siblings.

On the other hand, although I always had a good relationship with my sister, observing other adults that I knew and learning some of their intimate family stories, I got the impression that not too many of them had good relationships with their siblings, and very few of them, as adults, maintained the closeness and warmth that many of them had during childhood. In fact, many people I knew had very unhealthy relationships with their siblings, full of selfish behavior, taking advantage of each other, and having relationships contaminated with disappointments, insults, lack of responsibility, and worst of all, lack of mutual love and respect. To comfort myself in case my child were to end up an only child, I tried to convince myself that the benefit of that situation could be a life free of disappointments as a result of the negative effects of sibling relationships during both childhood and adulthood. We cannot choose our siblings, or any of our relatives, but we can choose really good and caring friends. So I told myself that this was what my daughter would have in her life: good friends. It was a classic example of sour grapes, but it helped me (and my daughter) to move past the "sibling obsession," at least to some extent. However, as my husband was not even close to accepting that attitude, he and I continued to having long and tiring conversations about the challenges of bringing up an only child, including the many disadvantages she would have, especially later in life when she would be an child with old (or relatively older) parents.

Rushing to the New Clinic; Cycle Monitoring in Clinic C

After the second IVF treatment in Clinic B which was canceled my husband and I were in a state of panic, and we agreed that we should start searching for the next clinic. At that time, another clinic (Clinic C) accepted us as patients, but the doctor wanted to do "cycle monitoring" before any protocol. Because I was still officially with Clinic B and waiting for another possible protocol there, I realized that doing parallel cycle monitoring in Clinic C and Clinic B would be beneficial, and I was eager to hear conclusions and recommendations from the doctor at Clinic C. That time was extremely busy and demanding for me. It consumed my whole life. I would have to go to Clinic C for cycle monitoring almost every day during the first two weeks of my cycle (from day one of the period until ovulation, on or around day fourteen). I often had to go to Clinic B for cycle monitoring on the same days that I went to Clinic C, as the doctors at Clinic B wanted to choose a "good-looking cycle" to proceed with the IVF protocol. Some conflicting lab results occurred while I was having blood work done at both clinics at the same time [see Elevated FSH, later in this chapter].

When the cycle monitoring was complete, Clinic C was willing to accept us for the IVF/ICSI protocol, but we decided not to go with that clinic. We had encountered contradictory references over the Internet; some people praised that clinic to the skies, while others condemned it. Our impression was that although the doctor appeared very knowledgeable, experienced, and kind, he was running clinics in several locations by himself. We didn't believe that he could properly cover all the professional demands necessary, as it appeared that all the clinics together would amount to a very large number of patients. But the main reason we decided not to go with Clinic C was that staff appeared extremely disorganized and unprofessional. The receptionist was typically unable to concentrate on her conversations with patients, as she constantly had to answer the phone at the same time; in addition, she gave incorrect directions, made mistakes with appointment times, and generally appeared "out of it" most of the time. Blood work was done almost in the middle of the corridor, with a lot of traffic constantly passing. During one blood draw, the technician simultaneously responded to and directed other patients who came through the corridor seeking information.

During the months that followed, we had consultations with a few doctors in some other IVF clinics. We still wanted so desperately to hear opinions from as many doctors as possible, as we hoped that we would hear some miraculous idea for how to treat our infertility problem, which might finally lead to a successful treatment and another pregnancy. We were also aware that not only were we seeking to choose a clinic, but that some clinics could refuse us. This actually happened, with two of the five clinics we went to offering us only the option of using the donor-egg protocol. I believed that in our situation, as I was running out of my reproductive time, we had to have an open door in at least one clinic while still receiving treated in another. I never regretted all that time spent in consultations with different doctors, because we heard a lot of explanations and opinions about our case and IVF in general, and that was the time when I learned the most. I did regret not having done IVF consultations with different clinics sooner. At the end of these consultations in the various clinics, all the doctors' conclusions were about the same and could be summarized in one sentence: knowing our infertility history, my age and diagnosis as a low responder, plus the male factor, which meant that we had to go through ICSI only, our chances for success with IVF would not be greater than 5 to 10 percent. Most of the clinics offered to do the "closure cycle," and if that was not successful, to continue with donor-egg protocols.

As I said, this was when I learned the most; in fact, I became extremely educated about IVF in general. Here are some questions and answers from my consultations with different fertility practitioners:

Q: Is it better to do a natural cycle without any stimulation?

A: Having a natural cycle is not a big difference because you are a low responder. Natural cycle doesn't make sense at your age. If you already have 90 percent of chromosomally abnormal eggs, you would need a minimum of ten natural cycles to catch just one healthy egg, and again, there is no guarantee even for that. At your age, the only approach would be to try to stimulate, and then to have five to ten eggs; out of that, maybe one would be good. There are women who have ten eggs at your age.

Q: What are the downsides of natural cycles?

A: If it is totally without any stimulation, it would be hard to determine precise ovulation time, and that would make it hard to calculate when it was thirty-six hours are after ovulation.

Q: How do you evaluate embryo quality?

A: If an embryo has eight cells on the third day after retrieval, it is a good indication that it may implant and develop. Eggs are considered to have good quality when they symmetrically divide into an even number of cells.

Q: Is it true that if there are more embryos in the culture medium that are later transferred, there is a better chance of implantation?

A: In the medium where the embryos are stored, they have some interaction, which helps them grow better.

Q: Do you think there may be an implantation problem in my case?

A: No. You don't have that problem, as you have already been pregnant.

Q: What is the maximum FSH that a woman can have and still undergo IVF?

A: We prefer if it is under 15, but we can tolerate FSH under 20. However, we are also looking at the antrafollicular number. The combination of FSH and the antrafollicular number is a parameter for deciding if we will proceed with that cycle or not.

Q: I was on the pill a few times prior to the treatment. Exactly what is the function of the pill?

A: The pill can prepare a cycle and control when the period will start. The pill decreases FSH. With older women, FSH rises even before the period starts, and then the follicles get the wrong message and don't grow simultaneously. So with the pill, follicles may grow more simultaneously, but it may be harder to trigger the system, because the pill may shut off the system. Sometimes we do give our patients the pill, and also the estrogen patch, in order to synchronize the follicles' growth at the same time.

Q: I noticed that all my cycles after the pill were very long, and my estradiol levels rose very slowly. Does it mean that if the pill is taken and one period is missed, the next one will have more eggs?

A: No, because follicles will be still produced, but because there will be no FSH around to trigger them, they will die. It means that whatever reserve you have is predetermined genetically.

Q: What are the health risks of taking too many gonadotropins and other medications? Can I get into early menopause because of too many IVF treatments?

A: No, there are no side effects. One study even shows that the percentage of cancer is decreased in IVF patients. No, you will not get into menopause prematurely, as there are a limited number of eggs released every month (fifty to a hundred), and this happens apart from the treatment. With the stimulation, we just try to get more mature eggs than the one that would occur naturally.

Q: What are the risks of my having early menopause because of repeated IVF protocols?

A: Theoretically, there is a risk of going through early menopause and losing ovaries, as ovaries need a minimum of three months to heal after the retrieval, and you have had so many repeated IVF protocols.

Q: What is the risk of my developing ovarian cancer?

A: The risk of ovarian cancer decreases with the pregnancy, because pregnancy results in less ovulation.

Q: Is my risk of ovarian cancer increased because I had stimulated ovulations with the repeated IVFs?

A: There are no indications of that.

Q: What can be done to improve sperm quality? Are there any supplements for better sperm quality? Are there any sperm tests to assess genetic content? To what extent does sperm quality influence embryo quality and conceiving probability?

A: Not too much can be done to improve sperm quality and quantity. Embryo quality is influenced 50 percent by sperm quality and 50 percent by egg quality.

Q: Should I be taking DHEA? What is the effect of DHEA, and is there any proved success with protocols when a woman takes DHEA? Is it true that the number of eggs is higher, but the quality doesn't improve and often decreases?

A: We support DHEA. We have had about a hundred patients take DHEA for four to five months prior to treatment, and we noticed some improvement. Eggs start to develop about every five to six months, so we advise our patients to take DHEA for a minimum of five months prior to the treatment.

Q: Is there anything else that a woman could take instead of, or in addition to, DHEA?
A: Nothing except DHEA, although there is no proof that it helps. Some clinics give something to improve blood flow, like baby aspirin. You can take vitamin E. Some clinics give antibiotics and progesterone after the retrieval.

Q: I read that the rate of aneuplody after ICSI is much higher (75 percent) than when done with traditional IVF (45 percent). Does it make sense in our case to do IVF without ICSI?
A: I don't believe those statistics. It might have been true in the early days of ICSI, as a result of damage of the egg, but not now when that technique has already been in use for about fifteen years.

Q: Is it possible to have a petri dish instead of ICSI at the final stage? Are there any better results if that part is left to nature?
A: That is called "rescue ICSI." Yes, it is possible to try first on a petri dish and then do ICSI, but that's risky because by the time it's possible to do ICSI, it may already be too late. Also, for eighteen years, studies have proved that there are better results with ICSI.

Q: What do you think about cytoplasmic transfer?
A: It is banned in North America.

Q: Will hormone replacement therapy help in my case?
A: No.

Q: Can my fertility be improved using our child's cord blood that has been taken and stored from her birth?
A: Not yet. It might be in the future, but not anytime soon.

Elevated FSH

My favorite explanation that I heard for FSH is that it is like a scanner. When scanning for eggs, a lower FSH number means that eggs were found more quickly; a higher number means that the scanner took longer to find them.

Most clinics go by the book, and if FSH is higher than 15, the doctors automatically suggest canceling IVF treatments with the woman's own eggs and proceeding with donor eggs, or at least canceling treatment during the cycle with elevated FSH. My FSH level was 10 at the age of thirty-nine, which was later explained to me as the threshold number, as FSH higher than 10 is an indicator of decreased fertility potential. However, my FSH started to rise rapidly as of my fortieth birthday, which was a textbook example and proof of the scientific theories and facts about rapid loss of fertility potential for women after certain age.

I had some concerns about the measuring method and timing of the FSH test. After a pause in the treatments, doctors in the clinic would usually give me prescriptions to have blood work done on the third day of my cycle, for testing FSH and other hormone levels prior to the next protocol. When I reviewed my previous blood work results, I realized that my FSH level was usually higher on day three than on day one or day two of the cycle. However, the first day of the cycle was defined differently from clinic to clinic. Some clinics define day one as the first day of full menstrual flow, which for some women is actually day two; other clinics consider day one to be the day of the first blood spot. If a patient's period started after clinic hours, in some clinics, the next working day would be counted as a day one. But for testing FSH levels, a difference of twenty-four hours, and even less time than that, could make a significant difference. For example, FSH could be 11 on day two, and then jump to 16 on day three, meaning that the doctor would consider a protocol with donor eggs instead of IVF with the woman's own eggs, and vice versa. Also, difference in FSH results may be caused by different measuring tools and methods. At one point I was conducting parallel cycle monitoring in two different clinics (B and C). It happened that the blood work results done at these two clinics on the same day gave two very different FSH results, with a discrepancy of greater than 30 percent. After that, I did a lot of research, and I realized that depending on the method of measurement (by humans or by machine), the results may differ. I decided to ask my family doctor for a prescription to monitor my hormone levels, including FSH, in order to be able to do my own screening.

My FSH levels were much lower when measured in cycles after the pill (Ovral, Minovral, etc.), which were prescribed occasionally when ovarian cysts were discovered by ultrasound during protocol monitoring. The doctors explained to me that after the pill intake, FSH levels measured in the next cycle were a much lower number, because of the previous pill intake, but this did not reflect the true FSH level. They further explained that once FSH is shown as elevated during one cycle, it is already a sign of diminished fertility, even if some future cycles show lower numbers.

I would recommend reading a book Inconceivable from Julia Indichova. The book is about a woman with significantly elevated FSH who succeeded getting pregnant naturally, with her own eggs when her FSH was 30.4.

Disasters Continue, or the Beginning of the End; Menopause Induction (Depo Lupron) Protocol in Clinic D

After waiting for months, we finally had an appointment with a doctor whom I will call "Doctor Miracle." Not only was he the first one not to mention donor eggs, but he also told us what we were actually hoping to hear: that the problem, after so many unsuccessful transfers of good-looking embryos (although low in quantity), might have been related to the implantation and the uterine lining. He suggested a biopsy of the uterine lining and a protein check. As per his explanations, if the results confirmed that some problem existed, it would indicate a possible embryo implantation problem. A protein tests would give us an answer, because an inappropriate level of proteins caused the embryo not to stick. He also wanted to conduct an Endometrial Function Test (EFT), which would determine if my endometrium was receptive to implantation. He explained that if the results of the uterine lining biopsy were not good, it could be fixed (in 80 percent of cases). The next step would be to put me into temporary menopause, with Depo Lupron, in order to allow the lining to regenerate. I could then undergo the IVF/ICSI protocol as soon as my period resumed. According to this doctor, such preparation might have tremendous results, and with the improved uterine lining, we might have a successful embryo implantation. (A more detailed explanation of the Depo Lupron protocol and medications used in the protocol can be found in the Appendix, under the List of Terms.)

I knew that I was making a big decision, and I had strong concerns that I might not ever recover from menopause. My concern was even greater for the fact that I was already forty-two, which was considered the last fertile year in the majority of IVF clinics. However, this doctor reassured us that, despite temporary menopause, my period would come again shortly after the menopause induction ended and that once that happened, I would be ready for the next IVF treatment. I did not blindly believe in that scenario, and I had concerns that my recovery might even be delayed by couple of weeks; if so, I would have wasted a lot of time. After a few days of thinking it over and discussing it with my husband, we decided to go with Depo Lupron preparation for the IVF protocol, despite the risks. The major reason for our decision was that we did not have too much to lose, and there was some hope that a completely new approach might bring positive results. Also, that clinic (Clinic D) did blastocysts on day five, and we were very interested in trying that, in order to learn if our embryos were capable of surviving until day five. There was also new job position that I had applied for, which put me under lot of stress, so it was perfect timing for me: I would be able to avoid IVF protocols during the job-interview process and the preparation for it. It turned out that being in an intensive artificial state of menopause for three months was actually much worse experience than going through the IVF protocol! It affected my physical well-being, my concentration and memory, and my mood; consequently, I didn't get the promotion.

It didn't take us long to decide to go with "Doctor Miracle." Did we regret it? Oh yes, mostly for the enormous amount of time we'd wasted and possibly the chances we'd lost. First, the biopsy of the uterine lining and the recovery lasted for about four weeks; the menopause stage lasted four months; and finally, the doctor didn't even want to start the protocol if my FSH was higher than 15, so we lost another three months until my FSH finally dropped. At last, eight months after we started with Clinic D, I had a complete IVF/ICSI treatment, which happened to be the worst and longest ever, with the worst-ever outcome.

Although my fear that the induced menopause would be prolonged or permanent did not come true, what happened was even worse than I could have imagined. For three full months, I was in a state of menopause: I felt awful, experiencing headaches, hot flashes, and mood swings. I wished for that condition to end as soon as possible, to be able to enjoy another few years before I reached natural menopause. I can easily say that of all the hormonal treatments, IVF/ICSI protocols, IUI protocols, follicle retrievals, embryo transfers, etc., this menopause induction was the most unpleasant, and any doctor told me to repeat it, I would probably decide never to go through it again.

My period didn't return immediately upon completion of menopause induction, as the doctor had predicted, but a month later. My FSH was 14. As of cycle day one, I started giving myself the prescribed shots of Suprefact 0.05, Repronex 75 units, and Puregon 375 units; after a few days, my estrogen was not only very low, but dropping. I was advised to cancel that treatment, which I did. The next period came in about thirty-five days. My FSH was 16, and the doctor didn't want to go ahead. The following period came after a regular twenty-six days, but my FSH was 17. Again, the doctor didn't want to proceed. Also, three big cysts were discovered, and the doctor was concerned about treating them. (Details about this protocol are summarized in the Table 2 in the Appendix, under the 9th protocol.)

So, at that time, we were not even going through unsuccessful treatments, but waiting for a good cycle, and having fears that a good cycle would never happen again. It's like when we look at photos of ourselves from ten years ago. At that time, we thought that we weighed too much and had too many lines on our faces, but now when look at those photos, we are amazed at how good-looking, young, and slim we really were! Similarly, I kept thinking about the "good old days" when I still had FSH levels low enough to start a protocol on any cycle!

A good cycle finally came! Or at least it appeared to be a good cycle. After more than six months of Depo Lupron preparation, all the while taking DHEA and for a while also taking the pill (Minovral) because of ovarian cysts, I was ready again. Somehow I had great hope for this cycle because it seemed similar to the one when I conceived our daughter: I was taking a pill prior to the cycle, and the protocol was at about the same time of year! (It was just six years later, when I was almost forty-three.) My medications were similar as in previous protocol, only this time I was taking increased amount of Puregon (400) and Repronex (150). (Details about this protocol are summarized in the Table 2 in the Appendix, under the 10th protocol.)

Every morning, I was assigned to a different ultrasound technician. There was some inconsistency with follicle numbers and measurements. For example, in the very beginning of my protocol, on day three, the technician measured nineteen follicles. By the next day, that number had dropped to eleven. Having such high number of follicles (nineteen) sounded like a miracle in my case, and I rather believed that technician who did the measuring on day three was inexperienced, counting some tissue that wasn't a follicle, or counting the same follicles twice. But deep in my soul I was feeling a tremendous joy thinking that unbelievably high number of follicles might have actually be the true numbers, that my agony with Depo Lupron preparation was worth and that Dr. Miracle was actually having a right approach. I was making an effort to suppress an enormous hope that this protocol which started with such an unexpected success will not get me pregnant.

Because I was on the pill prior to the protocol, the doctor expected the cycle to be slow (estradiol level to rise slower than usual); however, it was the slowest cycle ever. My estradiol finally got over 700, and it finally started to rise well on day fourteen of the cycle, the day in a normal cycle that would be the time for the egg retrieval. On day twenty-one of the cycle, my estradiol was almost 3,000, and there were five follicles, two of which were leading. On that day, my husband and I were more than convinced that retrieval had to be done no later than two days from that point, as the two leading follicles (2.3 cm. and 2.0 cm.) were very big (the other two were 1.7 cm. and 1.6 cm.). Also, we knew from our long past history that we could not expect more than two, maximum three, eggs to be retrieved. My gut feeling was that we should stick with the two leading follicles and that waiting for more eggs to mature would be just pushing the limit; we could risk losing the mature eggs. By that time, I had learned that if eggs overmature, they will not be fertile anymore. But the doctor's decision was to wait another day, continue the hormone therapy, and plan to do with the retrieval in three days instead of two. The clinic staff told us that he wanted to retrieve as many eggs as possible.

We had serious concerns about postponing for another day, and we asked to speak directly with the doctor. We wanted to discuss the matter with him and let him reassure us about our concerns, and we wanted to make him aware that we would not be willing to risk losing the best-looking follicles, with possibly healthy eggs, for retrieving a greater number of follicles with some, or even all, overmature eggs. We wanted to question that decision, but the doctor was unavailable and unreachable! We even went to the clinic and stayed in the lobby, in front of the elevator, so as not to miss a doctor, and to force him to meet with us if necessary, but he was already gone. And then, just as we feared, when four eggs were retrieved from five follicles and fertilized by implementing ICSI, for the first time ever, there were no embryos! What happened, most likely, was that the eggs overmatured. So not only did we burn a lot of money, but we probably lost at least two healthy embryos. And not only that—we might have lost our last potential future babies.

After that completely disastrous protocol, I was not sad, as I'd always been at the end of all the previous protocols: a total of fifteen-plus embryos transferred with the negative beta results. This time I was angry, with the doctor and with myself, because I had allowed him to trap me with his proposal, waste almost a year in menopause induction protocol preparation and taking lots of tests, and then, at the very end, possibly destroying our last chance by letting the eggs overmature. Up until the very end, I questioned my own opinion about that doctor. I had hoped that he would at some point actually show some hidden, miraculous IVF technique, proving that he was not just experimenting with me. I wish I had read comments about this doctor prior to making the decision to start IVF protocols with him. But who knows if I would have taken comments seriously at that time anyway. When we met him, he left a very good impression, and as many people mentioned on Internet blogs, he appeared to be very knowledgeable. Also, he offering an entirely different treatment plan, and he gave us hope. That was what we were looking for: hope. But then, during month after month of dealing with him, mostly while waiting for the IVF treatment to finally begin, we started to change our opinion of him. We suspected during the menopause-induction therapy prior to treatment that he was simply experimenting with me, but we tried to believe that he knew what he was doing. Unfortunately, the credit that we gave to him cost us a lot. Not only in wasted money, but also, most likely, in lost fertility time.

In a way, I was relieved when that never-ending nightmare with the Depo Lupron protocol and our experience with "Doctor Miracle" were over.

3

PUSHING THE LIMITS OF IVF

Secondary infertility was just as painful as not being able to conceive the first time. In some ways, it was actually worse the second time, because you knew what you were missing.

—Jill Sayre, *Waiting Womb*

Now on My Own

Eventually the time came when I felt that I was completely on my own. It was around my forty-third birthday: my husband had been without a job for a few months and he was in a deep depression about being jobless; even more than that, he was depressed because he didn't have the big family he had always dreamed about. He told me that he had lost all his enthusiasm and motivation for pursuing a career and money. He wasn't ready to give up his dream of a big family, despite his infertility; he wanted to have more kids, either adopted or with donor eggs. He eventually went through a very difficult midlife crisis. He even started to request to move from fertility treatments with my own eggs to protocols with donor eggs what was putting me under the additional stress. I wanted my baby, with my own genetic material. I felt like a rental womb for my husband to have kids, and I was very hurt by the fact that he totally ignored my feelings and desperation at not being able to have more of my own children. My husband's cruelty and total lack of compassion and gratitude for me, despite the fact that I was undergoing so many IVF/ICSI treatments because of his infertility, was a great disappointment for me, and a wake-up call about the nature of our relationship and the future. Although I strongly believed in marriage and family, and I was convinced that even the best marriages have big challenges and required a lot of tolerance, understanding, and flexibility between partners, I also knew that there was always a limit—and I was approaching it in my marriage.

At that time, the only joy in my life, and the only motivation for me to continue with IVF, was my daughter. I was aware that I belonged to the category of lucky IVF patients. But being aware of that didn't make me terminate IVF and give up on my dream for more

36

kids, especially when my husband insisted on having more kids with donor eggs. I felt I had reached a dead end and that the only way to save my marriage and family would be with more IVF/ICSI attempts to have another biological baby, as I wasn't comfortable with the idea of conceiving with donor eggs.

I was already doing intensive research on the Internet about cutting-edge fertility treatments and possible innovations that might have helped me. I even exchanged e-mails and arranged conference calls with some doctors abroad. I was desperately looking for the last hope, before I finally made the decision to give up IVF protocols with my own eggs. Based on the research, I decided to try a natural, low-stimulation IVF/ICSI protocol.

Turning to Natural IVF in Clinic E

Quod natura non sunt turpia. ("What is natural cannot be bad.") Latin phrase

The idea about natural IVF didn't come to me in one day. I had thought for a while that it might be a good idea to try a natural IVF cycle, or one with very low stimulation, and to rely on Mother Nature (except for the ICSI part which had to be done because of the male factor in our case). Wouldn't it be logical in the case of a woman who was a low responder to the fertility treatment stimulation, and still of theoretically fertile age, with possibly one healthy egg in the most cycles, to expect that the best approach for the fertility treatment would be just to go with the natural cycle and chase the one dominant healthy egg already preselected by Mother Nature? The natural IVF protocol had a potentially lower risk for failure of the IVF protocol, caused by the woman's hormonal system being unbalanced and destroyed by aggressive hormonal stimulation. Following that logic, the same woman might have a better chance for a healthy embryo formation, transplantation, and pregnancy.

The first time I asked my fertility doctor to try a low-stimulation IVF protocol, I was thirty-nine and still going to Clinic A. He refused to do it, maybe because I was still younger, fertility-wise, and there was some reasonable expectation that with the aggressive hormonal stimulation, I would produce more than two eggs.

I regretted that I hadn't looked for a clinic to do the natural IVF when I was younger. When I was forty, I had three IUI protocols on a natural cycles, without hormonal stimulation. At that time, my estradiol level easily went to the expected levels, and I had a healthy-looking egg. But at the age of almost forty-three, my estradiol level rose very slowly even with hormonal stimulation and did not reach the maximum levels it had attained when I was younger.

As I approached age forty-three, I found a clinic willing to do IVF/ICSI on natural cycles (Clinic E). Apart from being at risk that ovulation could occur before egg retrieval, everything else during natural IVF was better and more comfortable. I didn't have to go to the clinic as often as I did while undergoing hormonal stimulation, I didn't feel sick (as I did while I was under stimulation), I didn't have to inject myself with hormones several times a day, I didn't feel like I was a huge balloon, I didn't feel overwhelmingly hungry every hour of the day, and I didn't have abdominal pain and cramps (as I did while my stimulated follicles grew bigger). Also, there was less stress involved because nurses were not calling me every afternoon to tell me my hormone levels and give me instructions for that night's injection doses. I was more relaxed because I didn't know anything about my results between my visits to the clinic. I cared about the protocol, but somehow I was relying more on nature, not artificial stimulation, and so I was more ready to let go if I heard bad results.

Also, the cost of the treatment was about half. Although this didn't mean that at the end of the year we would end up with less money spent on IVF; on the contrary, it would have been even more expensive if the protocols were more frequent. At that time, the costs of the protocols were not even affecting my decision, as I felt that my biological clock was ticking toward not my last months, but my last days, of still being fertile, and I decided to do almost every cycle with natural IVF/ICSI. I felt that the money spent would be worth it because I was still trying to have my own baby, but at the same time, the natural IVF would have less negative impact on my present and future health. My objective was also that, with natural IVF, I would get a better picture of my real natural fertility status, I had hope that this would help me to arrive at the decision I would have to make in the near future: when to stop IVF altogether.

Addiction and Fiction

Just before I turned forty-three, I started going to the new clinic, Clinic E, the sixth one I'd gone to (counting the doctor's office where I did IUI and Clinic C, where I was doing just a cycle monitoring). I had a gut feeling that Clinic E would be the place where I would finally have another baby. I don't know why or how, but that feeling was in the air; it was love at first sight with the clinic, the doctor, and the staff. I loved the reception area and the big bright waiting room. For the sake of maintaining my mental and physical energy, as well as staying optimistic, I tried to see some good signs everywhere, even meaningless and superstitious one. This clinic was on the floor that was my lucky number, and it coincided with the number of my next attempt and with the date when I arrived in North America, starting my new life in a new world. Not only that, but on the very first day in the new clinic, my number on the waiting list was with the same as my daughter's birthday! There were "definite signs" for me that something good would happen in this clinic!

And then, something happened that surprised me. It was right around my forty-third birthday. I still had regular periods, but I heard some women a bit older than I was already complaining about missing periods for a few months. I noticed a first blood spot, and I felt tremendous joy! *Another one, thank God, there is another one!* I thought. The next day, I was on my way to the clinic for day two blood work and an ultrasound. The air was fresh, and the sky was cloudy, but it was not too cold for early morning in the fall. I walked the two blocks from the parking lot to the clinic, and I felt overwhelmed with happiness. *I am still going to a clinic!* I thought. *I'll soon see on the screen my little loving follicles again! I am going to see IVF doctors, nurses, lab technicians, and receptionists again!* I realized that going to the clinics had become an addiction for me, part of my life that I could not live without. And I couldn't help feeling the twilight of happiness for the hope I held, even if it was to last for just a few days before the doctors recommended cancellation of the IVF protocol.

Deep inside, I knew that I was at the peak of desperation. I knew that there was no more hope for me to have my own biological/genetic child, but in my soul and heart I was not ready to give up—or to move on. I wanted to continue to go to the clinic, to sacrifice almost all the rest of my normal life, all my plans and ambitions, just so that hope would never die.

Fertility Milestone: My Forty-Third Birthday

During the year before I turned forty-three, I felt very stressful about that number, as that was the age when most fertility clinics stopped treating women with their own eggs. I remembered all the previous birthdays, Christmases, and New Years; I always thought that something would finally happen during the following year of my life or during the next calendar year. As my forty-third birthday approached, I still had tiny hope, however small, that something might happen; but I knew it was more likely that nothing would happen, except more and more tiring treatments, negative results, stress, depression, wasted time, ruined career, and financial loss.

I started thinking that I should stop torturing myself and come up with some parallel plan, or a "contingency plan," as one author recommended in her book. I remembered I realizing long ago, while still in my twenties, that most satisfaction and happiness in life depends on our perception and ability to be happy. Put two people into the same situation, and one may feel extremely happy while the other will feel extremely miserable. I didn't think that my situation had the potential for either extreme happiness or extreme misery, but I saw myself leaning toward considering everything that happened as tragic. What about sick people who are still full of energy and passion for life? What about poor people, people living in war zones, people surviving hurricanes, earthquakes, other natural disasters, and/or horrible accidents? Their lives were extremely difficult, but many of them still lived their lives and found ways to be happy. How could I compare myself to any of them?

I asked myself to anticipate how I would feel two, five, or teen years from what was then the present time. I tried to imagine the worst-case scenarios, and I believe that my imagination might have helped me in my decision-making process for the future. I anticipated the questions I might ask myself in the future, such as: "Why didn't I do this?" or "Why did I do that?" Then I asked myself what I could do at that very moment in order to have no regrets in the future. But after that whole exercise, I had only one clear answer, and it came from my heart. I still wanted another child, and I still wanted him or her to be my genetic/biological child. I still could not accept the idea of a donor-egg baby.

And then my birthday arrived. Forty-three. I believed that on my birthday I would be in a state of such a depression that I would want to continue sleeping for the rest of the day. I was surprised when I woke up in an extremely good mood. Instead of crying while I driving to work, I loudly sang my favorite song and enjoyed the nice sunny day. And somehow I felt enlightened deep in my soul with the belief that something good must happen during the next year and that I must move on. The previous night, I had watched a movie by Claude Lelouch, *Les Uns et les Autres*, and I felt deeply touched and reminded that life goes in cycles and that we cannot escape our destiny.

At that time, I read another explanation of the female fertility potential. Imagine a bucket full of apples. When apples are just picked from the tree, they are fresh and healthy; but the longer the apples sit in the bucket, the more rotten apples there will be. Apples are like a woman's eggs. When a woman is young, all her eggs are fresh and healthy. When her fertility starts to decline, some eggs become like those rotten apples. But sometimes, much to our surprise, we find in the bucket full of rotten apples one untouched, healthy, and beautiful apple. How often does that happen? Not very often. But I still had hope that it would happen to me.

Yes, indeed, I had to go to the clinic that same morning for my natural IVF protocol. I kept my thoughts optimistic, telling myself that there was no reason to be convinced, as I almost entirely was, that after the last failed IVF protocol, I had no fertile eggs anymore, and that hope was lost forever. I was even thinking that the perfect name for my baby, if a girl, would be Hope. If ever born, that child would be the gift of my boundless faith and hope.

And on that day, my mother called with birthday wishes. She then asked me if she had ever told me a story from her early career as a doctor, when a woman about fifty years old came to see her, complaining of all sorts of problems, which another doctor had treated as stomach problems. And it was my mother who discovered that the woman was already five months pregnant! This touched me deeply. My sweet mommy just wanted to believe that same miracle would happen to me, and she wanted that baby for me with all her heart—to see me happy, but also to see me finally stop ruining my health and life with IVF!

Egg Retrieval/Embryo Transfer on Easter; Last Trust in God

In Clinic E, I was doing only "natural IVF" cycles with very low stimulation. The doctor chose to go with an agonist/antagonist protocol. Typically, I was taking a very low dose of Puregon, Menopur, or Repronex (100 units) and GnRH antagonist Cetrotide or Orgalutran. And I underwent a natural, low stimulation IVF protocol during my each cycle for about six months! (Details about my IVF protocols in Clinic E are summarized in the Table 3 in the Appendix. A more detailed explanation of the natural low stimulation protocol and medications used in the protocol can be found in the Appendix also, under the List of Terms.)

During the cycle, apart from clinic testing, which was not performed as often as on the high-stimulation IVF protocols, I regularly checked my mucus and ovulation with the fertility monitor. According to the fertility monitor, my cycles each looked good; "textbook" examples, as the clinic staff would say. I was already forty-three, but during every cycle, the fertility monitor showed a few days of fertile time and one to two days of ovulation time. The irony was that, according to the fertility monitor, I was doing great, almost like a twenty-five-year-old woman with regular periods.

And there was a protocol around Easter. Everything went well and smoothly. Under the natural, low-stimulation IVF protocol, I even had three eggs retrieved from four follicles! And out of three eggs, two were fertilized, and I had two embryos for transfer!

I had turned to God after so many years. During my growing-up years in a communist country, I was raised to be an atheist, and only during my early childhood did I believe in God and sense that God existed somewhere. During the natural IVF protocol, I was in need of help, and I wanted to turn to God and ask Him to look at me and my life, to help me to feel special and happy, as the way I felt when I was a child. But it was too late. My eggs were probably too old, and the protocol didn't work, and I finally accepted that it never would.

Advocating for Natural IVF Protocol in Low-Responding Women

Given all my knowledge, experience, and known outcomes of the IVF protocols, if I could have the chance to turn back time and choose to repeat some IVF protocols and skip others, I would certainly skip the Depo Lupron menopause-induction protocol, and I would probably choose to go with only natural IVF protocols, without any hormonal stimulation at all or with very low stimulation. I would probably even go without the hormonal injections that were supposed to control ovulation, taking the risk of ovulating and losing only one egg, in the case that any IVF clinic would accept to deal with 100 percent nonstimulated protocol. The other option that I might have chosen would be the agonist/antagonist protocol with Menopur and prior DHEA preparation [*see* last protocol in Clinic B].

I believe that there are certain benefits to the IVF protocol without stimulation for women who are low responders, as I am. In my case, without any prestimulation, or with just a very light one, I produced one egg; with the huge doses of gonadotropins, my maximum production was two to three eggs. This led me to conclude, following all the years of experience with IVF, that it would have been prudent for me to leave everything to nature, and during each good-looking cycle, just do the natural IVF protocol. Which actually would have meant just doing the final part as an IVF procedure: egg retrieval, ICSI, and embryo transfer, as these steps were necessary because of the male infertility factor. When I started new IVF protocols after my daughter was born, I thirty-nine, I probably still had a few good cycles each year; that is, cycles that still had fertility potential. If I underwent cycle monitoring at that time, the doctors would have picked the good cycle and then proceeded with the natural IVF. In my opinion, for me, as a low responder, such an approach would have given me a greater likelihood of conceiving.

With just natural IVF, followed by ICSI, I would have avoided the scenario where my body's hormonal system was most probably getting wrong messages because of all the different, frequent, and usually aggressive hormonal stimulation, causing my eggs to not develop properly and to not become healthy, surviving embryos. During some protocols, as a result of the hormonal "mess," my body was also probably not properly prepared to receive an embryo and keep it alive. Going through the natural protocol, I was able to have a better sense of my cycle; I could tell if it was a good cycle, or one that required a lot of assistance. My feeling, not necessarily a scientifically correct one, was that if the cycle was slow moving, the follicle slow growing, and the estradiol level lazily increasing, that cycle would have failed anyway. Because my previous hormonally stimulated IVF protocols were chosen randomly, nobody would ever have evidence if the cycle chosen for IVF treatment was naturally predetermined to lead to healthy eggs/embryos, or just a sloppy one, which every healthy woman occasionally has, and which all women have more frequently as they age. It might have happened that in some of my IVF treatments, no medication could have helped a cycle that was naturally predetermined to fail to become a fertile one, and in that case, all stimulation and IVF was done in vain. But also it might have happened that the drugs might have improved the quality of a cycle and thus might have multiplied my chances. Nothing is for sure, and doctors certainly have their own opinions on that. But I have a strong feeling that, for me, natural IVF would have been the best solution. If I had to pick what I most regret doing during my IVF journey, it would be that I didn't start the natural, low-stimulation protocols earlier.

Traveling around the Planet to Buy Hope; Investigating Cytoplasmic Transfer in Turkey

I still could not completely give up the idea that somewhere, somehow, there was an IVF method that might help us. While surfing the Internet I found information on the cytoplasmic transfer, which was described as:

> *Still an experimental method in assisted reproductive technology (ART), fertility technique whereby cytoplasm from a donor egg is injected into an egg with compromised mitochondria. The resulting egg is then fertilized with sperm and implanted in a womb, usually that of the woman who provided the recipient egg and nuclear DNA.* (https://en.wikipedia.org/wiki/Cytoplasmic_transfer)

In North America, cytoplasmic transfer was prohibited, as federal laws claim that genetically manipulated embryos constitute a "biological product." But I found a country where cytoplasmic transfer might possibly be performed: Turkey. And I have found reputable clinic in Istanbul. My husband and I had some e-mail correspondence with the lead doctor from the Istanbul clinic. We decided to give it a try. It was also a good excuse to visit that gorgeous city for the first time.

When I arrived at the airport, the administrator from the clinic and the driver welcomed me. The administrator assigned to me was a very nice and kind young woman. She chatted with me on our way from the airport to the clinic. When we arrived at the clinic, despite the very late evening hours, the lab technician was waiting for me. It was important to have my blood work done so that the results would be available for my appointment with the doctor the following day. Then the administrator explained what a needed to know about the appointment with the doctor on the following day, she gave me a cell phone and the driver took me to a hotel close to the clinic, where they already had reserved a room for me.

The clinic, to my surprise, looked very differently than clinics in North America. The clinics that I went to in North America were mostly leased spaces in medical buildings close to major highways, or in office buildings downtown, close to the subway. This clinic was a sole tenant in a three-story building built in an old-fashioned architectural style. There was a big open space on the ground floor, with a reception area that looked more like a hotel lobby, complete with armchairs, a TV, and even a small restaurant. I was pleasantly surprised by the beauty, neatness, and modernity of the clinic interior, which did not resemble a medical facility. I was very pleased with the warm welcome I received from the clinic's kind and professional staff. I almost felt like a celebrity, and for a moment I forgot that I was just one fertility patient, after having been in so many North American clinics, where there was hardly a chair to sit on in the lobby, open garbage boxes filled with sanitary pads, and dirty paper sheets on the examination tables; not to mention the clinic staffs there, which were, if not extremely unpleasant, at least usually showing no empathy or kindness toward the fertility patient, as if the battle with infertility was little more than an annoyance rather than one of the biggest problems that a woman, man, couple may experience in life.

I will never forget my first appointment with the doctor in Turkey. That morning was magically bright, and I sat in the car, looking out at hilly Istanbul. It was spring, the sky was clear, there were flowers all around, and a chestnut tree was blooming. I was extremely happy that my first appointment with the doctor had to be in the other branch of the same clinic, located in the part of Istanbul that sits on the continent of Asia. I had the opportunity to see so much of the city while making the long ride across the Bosporus. But what excited me the most was the fact that as part of my struggle to have a second child, I would be on three different continents during a period of less than twenty-four hours: from North America to Europe and onward to Asia! I saw that as a good sign that a miracle might happen.

Finally, I stepped on the ground of Asia for the first time in my life and entered the Asian branch of Istanbul clinic. After a very short wait time, I met with the doctor. He was extremely professional, kind, and charming. It impressed me how much he knew about our case, which he had read thoroughly. He well understood our IVF history, which we had provided through the e-mails. I had the impression that he had vast knowledge and experience with ART, which by that time, with all my previous experience, I could already gauge when talking to different ART practitioners. He discussed some different options with me, explaining all the avenues that I could consider, none of which was with donor eggs. Donor-egg protocols were banned in Turkey, because that method was not approved by the Islam. However, per my expectations, given my previous history with IVF, this doctor did not suggest any miracle successes. There were still some results that he needed to review, and then we would talk more about a possible protocol in the next few days.

I finally had some time for sightseeing. The most magical moment in Istanbul, for me, was when a Muslim priest would call for prayer from the minaret of the mosque, his voice echoing melodically. Everyone would stop to listen to the call for prayer, and then they would not move until the prayer was over. It was such an amazing experience to be stopped for few times during the daily rush, and to remember where we belong in the wide spectrum of life, what our purpose and values in this life are. And also, to be reminded of the tiny moment in the vast universe that has been given to us, to remember to be happy and not to waste a moment. And finally, to be reminded of God, no matter what our religion, to feel awed by the sacred, creative power. For me, that was belief in destiny and the cycle of events, causes, reasons, punishments, and rewards. I felt very spiritual while I was in Istanbul, and I wished that we, who live in the Western world, could find some similar way to remind ourselves daily of the most important things in life, instead of living day by day, rushing madly to achieve goals and objectives that are not always important and are predominantly materialistic.

Upon release of some test results, I waited to have my final appointment with the doctor. In the meantime, I read the interviews with him in the local magazines; I saw articles about the gala parties and fundraising that he and his clinic staff organized for different reasons. I got the impression that he was a big star and celebrity in Istanbul, not just for ART, but for other reasons as well. I also got the impression that a great number of people learned about ART through this doctor, rather than through ill-informed journalists and members of the media, as was the case in North America. And I also had the impression that fertility patients were treated by him and his staff as very special people, who were suffering a great deal, despite the fact that they had no actual illness. While a patient in North American clinics, I missed such an attitude from the clinic staff.

I could have decided to arrange for the protocol with application of cytoplasmic transfer, as long as I would come to Istanbul for monitoring, and then, when I had a good cycle, the protocol would start. It was left to me and my husband to decide on that. But upon leaving the clinic and Istanbul, I knew that it was too late. Again, it was confirmed for me that no ART method in the world could overcome a woman's age. I only regretted that I hadn't explored the opportunity of cytoplasmic transfer earlier, when I still had-good looking embryos. And I greatly missed having the opportunity to be treated by the doctor in the Istanbul clinic.

4

HARDSHIPS OF IVF CLOSURE

Man is the only animal that laughs and weeps; for he is the only animal that is struck with the difference between what things are and what they might have been.

William Hazlitt

Wanting to Get My Life Back and to Live Happily Ever After

I've heard it said that victory belongs to those who want it most and stay in the fight the longest. I agree that is true as a rule, but I would also say that the infertility battle is an exception to that rule.

Throughout my life I have had to make many difficult decisions: what profession to choose, who to choose as my life partner, whether to immigrate to North America. But deciding to stop fertility treatments was definitely the most difficult decision of my entire life. Although at certain point it became if not obvious, at least very probable, that I wouldn't succeed in having more children, either naturally or with the help of IVF, I felt deep sadness and reluctance regarding making the decision to stop the IVF treatments. I felt as if not having more kids wasn't a decision made of my own free will. In addition, I couldn't comfort myself by saying that this, like everything else, was God's will, because, as a person born and raised in communist country, I was an atheist. It would have been much easier for me if my husband had been the one to make the decision about IVF closure, but he was not willing to accept that we would have only one child. And the IVF clinics never made the decision; they left it up to the patients to decide when to opt for IVF closure. I've described all this previously, I realize, but it's important for me to emphasize how alone I felt—and how overwhelming it was to have to bear sole responsibility for making this decision, the hardest one of my life.

As I'd done before, I thought of the future, asking myself questions and trying to imagine myself in a few years, older and without any chances to conceive. I tried to anticipate

46

what I would say and how I would feel at that time, and most important, what I would regret having done—or not done—regarding my fertility treatments. This exercise was very difficult, as it would be in any aspect of life, but it was useful and helpful. (In general, people would be happier and more successful if they did similar mental exercises more frequently, as this would help them make important decisions.)

As I've said, I was concerned that I already had a higher risk for health problems, although no IVF clinic or doctor ever confirmed that exposure to IVF might lead to a higher risk of illness. My general health was very good between protocols. But I started anticipating that it might not be that way forever and that I was playing with the fire by exposing my body to an increased risk for cancer or another deadly disease. In some cancer patients, the disease might not be readily apparent while the body is still strong, and a healthy person may be able suppress symptoms for a long time, leading to the risk of late diagnosis. Again, I do not base this on medical or scientific facts; it is simply my own opinion. Nevertheless, I worried that I was at risk. I started asking myself if I had the right to continually expose myself to such an elevated risk, especially when I had a child who depended on me. It was my responsibility as a mother to take care of myself, for my daughter's sake even more than my own. These thoughts plagued me, and I started imagining my own funeral and hearing people's comments: "Yes, she was crazy to have all those treatments! Why would she do that? She is the one to blame for this poor kid not having her mother now." Not that I cared what people would say, but I knew that in this instance they would be correct. Knowing that these comments I imagined would be right to some extent really bothered me. I started feeling more responsible for my future decisions about IVF, hoping that it wasn't already too late to avoid the eventuality of health problems, even premature death, which I dreaded.

We were also concerned about our huge financial debt. We would have to live in a very small, old house, and we would not be able to take vacations overseas for years. During the IVF years, despite the fact that our debt was rising exponentially, I almost never allowed myself to feel stressed about the financial aspect of the treatments. I believed that it was completely fair for my husband to carry that burden entirely, especially because I contributed my fair share of income by working full-time continuously throughout our marriage prior to IVF and during the IVF time as well. I was always convinced that no matter how much debt we ended up with, even if we were forced to downsize close to the poverty level, all the sacrifice would be worth it if we finally had more children.

One thing that did upset me was the wasted time. How many other things could I have done during the time I spent in IVF? How much more time could I have spent with my child? (By that I mean more relaxed time, when I was not always in rush, usually because of IVF, as well as working full-time.) How many of my other dreams might I have fulfilled? I'd had so many ideas and dreams, but I had hardly time to even try to turn some of them into reality.

So there I was, with all these thoughts and feelings swirling through my head and heart, just as my forty-fourth birthday approached. It was on my birthday that I decided to end the infertility battle. I realized that there were only six years before I turned fifty, and that was a number that scared me. Maybe that seems harsh, but three of my four grandparents died in their early fifties, and when I was young, "fifties" represented the age when was not unexpected for people to die. I recalled my past birthdays, thinking about events in my life from my the time I turned thirty until the time I turned forty, and I realized how much my inner being had changed during that period, how many changes and achievements had occurred. But I also realized how quickly those years had passed, and how many plans and dreams didn't come to fruition. It felt like other things—more often than not IVF had pushed them aside, forcing them to wait for some future time that I realized now might never come.

When I finally made a firm decision to cancel any further fertility treatments, I wasn't sure that I wouldn't ever wonder if I should have tried "one more time." Mostly, my very strong bond with and love for my daughter helped me to cope with these feelings. Having so much more time to spend with her made me entirely happy. Focusing on how much I enjoyed my time with my daughter, I tried to convince myself that if I had a new baby to take care of now, I would lose this precious time with my daughter, and she would already be a grown girl by the time I would be able to devote my attention to her again.

As soon as I finally decided to stop IVF, I felt tremendous relief. I was blessed to have a child; I was a healthy woman, a successful professional, a middle-class citizen. I also happened to love and be married to an infertile man. Because of difficult life circumstances, we had delayed having kids. And we were not well informed about infertility in general and our infertility. All these things were just part of the way life had played out. Why did I keep asking for more than I could have? It was time to finally start enjoying life after struggling with infertility for seven years.

That year was the start of a new era: life without clinics, protocols, injections, retrievals, false hopes, and disappointments. I was able to spend more time with my daughter, and that brought me great joy. But regardless, I knew that, until the end of my life, I would always feel a silent sadness for not having more children and that whenever I saw a pregnant woman or a newborn baby, I would always have to look away.

Marital and Family Crisis; Emotional Roller Coaster

We are born alone, we live alone, we die alone. Only through our love and friendship can we create the illusion for the moment that we are not alone.

Orson Welles

I was ready "to live happily ever after"; my husband wasn't.

After the Depo Lupron menopause-induction protocol, when I suffered the most and had my first-ever protocol without one single embryo transferred, it became obvious that we would not succeed with IVF. At that time, after the first obvious failure of IVF, my husband started to aggressively pressure me to begin a donor-egg protocol. He also initiated some very nasty and cruel conversations, which continued for another few years.

As I've stated, my husband could not accept the fact that we would have only one child, especially because there were other avenues to explore through IVF—namely, donor-egg protocols—and he became obsessed with pursuing this. He was totally consumed with the idea of having not just another baby, but twins with donor eggs.

Lack of mandatory counseling in the clinics and the general attitude toward the donor-egg program in the clinics definitely reinforced my husband's attitude and position. Whenever anyone in any clinic mentioned the donor-egg option, the manner and tone of the conversation indicated that conceiving a baby with donated eggs was a natural and prudent thing to do. Even if rationally thinking it was the most prudent thing to do in our case, it certainly was not natural in our case or in any case, and it was not easy for me to accept. And I am certain that if the clinics had been more careful in explaining that option to couples, respecting and understanding the complexity of that choice in general and its impact on each couple individually, my husband wouldn't have bought into the idea so completely, fixating on it as absolutely the only way to go. Or at least he would have understood the complexity and difficulty of that decision for me, as a woman who had already suffered many years of undergoing IVF because of her husband's infertility, who at the end was supposed to have another of her own biological/genetic children, not a child conceived with just her husband's genetic material and some other woman's donor egg. My husband even told me that one of the doctors once had to keep from laughing in my face when I asked about trying another few times before using the donor-egg program.

In the last years of my IVF that same IVF industry was very vocal about donor egg option. However, during the 7 years, or at least at the time when I was still able to conceive naturally, it was never recommended that we proceed with IVF or IUI with donor sperm, or any other option with my own eggs. During the first years of IVF, when I was still under the age of 40, the IVF industry did not give us information and predictions how or what we can expect in future (only donor egg protocols). Nobody ever worn me that if IVF with my own eggs fails over the years, I will be almost obliged to proceed with the donor egg IVF protocol, and everyone in IVF industry will believe that it would be most prudent thing to do, having my husband on their side. I feel that it was very unfair and I was discriminated as a woman. My husband recognized this and used it against me. It would be unrealistic to expect from IVF doctors and clinic staff to get into the deeper analysis and concerns about impacts of struggle with infertility on partner relationships, but that is a reason why each clinic should have mandatory counseling. Counselors have the expertise to recognize challenges of infertility on couples and help them through the process.

Although I am not a religious person, I was disturbed about thinking that I could create a human being in any manner other than the reproductive ability that nature gave us. That ability gives us the right to create babies, tiny human beings that resemble us, along with the opportunity to find meaning and purpose in life through our children and family and to take responsibility for that unique and precious creatures on this planet, our child(ren), through whom each of us human beings will live on eternally, as our child(ren) will have children who will have children, and so on. I had butterflies in my stomach just thinking of a donor-egg baby in my womb, conceived through egg donation from an anonymous donor found through the Internet or a clinic database. The idea of creating a human being from a completely unknown woman and my husband, bearing it in my womb, and then giving birth to it was utterly alien to me. I couldn't imagine that I would be able to feel the same way toward that baby as I would toward my own child, created with my genes, as well as my husband's. Through all the IVF years, I never thought of using donor eggs as an option; my motivation for going through IVF was not merely to have more any kids, but to have more of *my own children.* My husband's urgent desire for donor-egg babies forced me to think about that option, and it was very difficult for me to feel comfortable with that idea. If I could not have children of my own at all, I would have probably decided to do the donor-egg protocol, but as I already had a child of my own, I could not be certain that I could even love these human beings created with donor eggs. For me, the only acceptable scenario would have been to have a known egg donor. But I did not have any female friends young enough to still be of an age of high fertility, and my sister was only two and half years younger than I. Even if she wanted to become my donor, there would probably be a very slim chance that her eggs would be any better than mine. I thought about one of my cousins, who was five years younger than I, but my husband did not want her as a donor; he preferred having an anonymous donor.

And being uncomfortable about the idea of donor egg baby was not the only reason why I could not accept that idea. What looked threatening for me was my vision of the future. At that time, when I started seeing my husband's nature and nature of our relationship in different light and more objective, I had a vision of very probable future life, not based on my paranoia, but based on past experience. I was pretty sure that my husband would request from me to keep the fact about our donor egg child or children as an absolute secret. He would insist that nobody in the world knows the truth as that would be the best for our family. And if he suspects that I was telling anyone, he would accuse me of being a selfish mother not carrying for our childrens' interests and our family reputation. I saw my future and myself as a piece of furniture in his household, first as a rental womb, then as a "contracted out mom" for his kids, as a woman who from looking outside, lives in the modern world and modern family, but actually lives totally humiliated as in Dark Ages. There was a great risk for me to believe that he, who always mastered scenarios which will work best for him and protect best his own interests, would act any different, even if I gave birth to his kids conceived with donor eggs. And that he wouldn't continue to live as a "couch potato" in our household and still not feel bad about me being under so much work, stress and household duties. And he would be enjoying the rest of his life in complete happiness as an "alpha male", appearing from the outside as a perfect family man who can care and provide for his three (minimum) kids and even for his elderly parents. He was planning to sponsor them to live in North America with us. Such a fulfillment and legacy! But the fact that my husband in past and present time did not show signs of selflessness, care for me, respect for me, flexibility, tolerance, help in everyday life and so on and that such a scenario for his happiness had to be almost entirely on my expense, while at the background I would have to be a work-horse, without much appreciation and without fulfilment of my own life dreams and priorities, drew me far from it.

I was still open to the option of a surrogate baby, but under the condition that my husband took the lead in Plan B: a surrogate child. I had enough of life with IVF, and I did not want my future life to be all about the surrogate baby. This time, I wanted my husband to do all the work! But my husband was not willing to consider a surrogate child because, in his opinion, it would have not been "socially acceptable." In other words, with that solution, he wouldn't be able to cover up our failure. With the donor-egg option, only we and God would know that the child or children were genetically his but not genetically mine, and apparently, that scenario was the one he preferred. Or he perhaps he didn't want to take on the responsibilities and duties for pursuing Plan B, as well as the future responsibilities and possible risks involved with having surrogate child or children. For him, it was much easier to continue pressuring me to conceive with donor eggs. He kept telling me, "Genes are not everything. You don't want to give birth to our daughter's sibling!" He even had the nerve to say, "I can't believe that you went through fertility treatments for seven years, but you didn't ever have a Plan B!"

That last statement floored me. Not only did my husband, expect me to go through IVF for seven years, (without even showing appreciation for me going through IVF because of his sterility), he also expected that I should have developed a Plan B to succeed in having more kids and that I should have started working on it while still undergoing IVF! I simply could not believe it. It was so unfair to expect me to be the one to develop a Plan B while I was also the one aggressively undergoing IVF, having a baby and taking care of a little child, working full-time, commuting to work for two hours each day, and doing all the household chores! And I was not only supposed to develop a Plan B, but to be enthusiastic about it, despite my deep disappointment and sadness for not having more kids, even after seven years of intensive battle with infertility!

At that time, I started feeling that this person, who unfortunately happened to be my husband, was so deep into his own pathological misery and dissatisfaction with life that he not only tried to put all the blame on me, but also expected me to resolve the situation. I almost felt like I had to apologize for the desire to take care of my health and devote myself to our child. I felt guilty and responsible for not developing a Plan B, for not finding a way to fulfill my husband's obsession with the idea of a big family, for not making him happy and keeping our family together.

"You are the one to break this family, not me, and you are doing it to your child!" he told me. "You are the one to be blamed for what happened to you, since you believed that I would accept that we would have only one child. That's your problem, not mine. You are the woman who, until the age of forty-three, didn't realize that she was a woman."

My husband's attitude and behaviour soon made it obvious that he wouldn't easily drop the idea about the donor-egg protocol. On a daily basis, he intensely demanded that I conceive with donor eggs so that our daughter would not become "handicapped" as an only child with no siblings. He kept accusing me that it would be selfish of me if I do not do it, that I would be "punishing" our child. I constantly heard accusations, threats, and ultimatums. "Your life may be over and destroyed, but our daughter's life is just beginning. What is important for her future is not so much to be with her mother, but to have someone close to her age for the rest of her life." He also told me, "You are not able to provide me with a family. I will never give up on my dream of a big family. The essence of being human is to satisfy the ancient desires which give motivation for life. If I don't have more kids, I'll slowly die. I can stay motivated to be a family provider only if I know that I am providing for someone. But my problem is solvable because I am a man!" And then he accused me of choosing to be a loser in life. And at that moment, I started feeling that by deciding to love and marry an infertile man, a man who is treating me with such a cruelty, I did end up being a loser.

I was totally broken with the feeling that I made such a mistake in life to love and marry an infertile man who did not share the same feelings for me. For that mistake I was paying a huge price for going through IVF (despite the fact that I was perfectly fertile). But the worst price I had to pay was the fact that I had taken up in life with an infertile man and therefore as a consequence I sacrificed more kids of my own.

The two years that followed were the worst nightmare of my life. I realized that it was not hard to destroy happiness, but it was hard to preserve it. Perhaps preserving happiness is the hardest thing of all to truly accomplish. I felt broken, and I no longer saw any meaning in life; I was left with nothing but feelings of deep humiliation. My daughter was the only thing that kept me going. I just wanted to fall asleep and wake up with my old life: happiness, peace of mind, motivation, optimism, enthusiasm, and so on. I had always loved life; for most of my life, I was happy, active, and full of energy. Prior to this crisis, I could hardly remember ever feeling truly depressed. However, when IVF closure happened, I was so distraught that I cried several times every day. I couldn't eat, I couldn't sleep, and I was afraid that I would die of sheer stress. I lost interest in almost everything in life, and I had to force myself to function normally. I wanted solitude, and I tried to be close to nature in order to bring myself back to the basics of life and to enjoy very simple things. At that time, it was very difficult for me to live close to my husband because it exposed me to cruel accusations and blame for our child being an only child. To have only one child was not what I had wished for, and I don't think too many women could have tried harder to have more children.

I realized that I lived in IVF bubble and also in the love bubble. I loved my husband a lot, I trusted him and I was voluntary doing many things in our life together, not only for my own happiness, but sometimes even more for his. But being selfless back-fired me. I felt deeply sad, disappointed, and angry that all the sacrifices I made were for the wrong man, a man who didn't deserve any of it, a man who didn't truly love and respect me, and who didn't even care about me and my well-being. If he had only shown some appreciation, care, and empathy, it would have compensated for my loss. But he showed none.

And to make it clear: my despair was not for the lost love. Maybe in the very beginning of "crisis" I was in total shock with the feeling that my husband absolutely didn't love me and didn't care for my feelings, my well-being and my life and I was very hurt. Apart from the great emotional shock of feeling that my husband did not need me anymore and did not have any interest in staying with me because I was not able to provide him more kids, and the only way to keep him and our family together would be to conceive with the donor-egg protocol, I also had some ego issues. I realized that my husband and the father of my child had dumped me, as if I had an expiration date, and he was willing to stay with me only if I accepted being "a rental womb" for his, but not my, genetic babies. And it took me a while to adjust my own feelings so that I do not get emotionally involved with someone who far back in the past stopped being emotionally involved with me, although I hadn't realized it until the time of IVF closure. However, my biggest despair was for the lost investment that I made, which happened to be a huge investment, involving the most precious that a woman and a human being may have: my health, my personal time and my time with my child, my career and possibly even my biological kids. And other investments of less value for me, such as higher standard of living and better social status, career promotions, as well as other interests, hobbies, and activities. And I was desperate not only for the fact that it happened to be a wrong investment, but also for all the problems in present and future that were created.

And despite the fact that I was living in the Western world, in the twenty-first century, I also felt that my husband's attitude, as well as the attitude of the entire IVF industry, had put me back in the Dark Ages. I felt like a woman with no rights, no freedom, no voice, and no one to help me get myself out of the cruel situation.

For the prolonged time I felt like a complete failure and a loser, as a person, as a mother, as a professional, as a woman. I felt that I hadn't done anything distinguished, and I hadn't accomplished anything in my life, as an intellectual, a professional, or a free spirit. I realized that I wasn't respected at work, and that I was treated as a mediocre professional. In my spare time, for many years I was not reading or educating myself; I was not engaged in any activities of with spiritual value. I hadn't pursued my dreams of writing, teaching, traveling, or owning a small business! I was not involved in volunteer or community work, I was not helping people in need, and I was not living for any good cause. For seven years, there was nothing in my life other than coping with infertility and regular daily work at my workplace and at home. With the exception of the time spent with my child and caring for her, I have been leading a completely materialistic and meaningless life for years.

And as a woman, I felt old, tired, and sick of life. IVF and my husband deprived me of my ability to be happy. I felt that if I die tomorrow, there will be no damage to this world; even my child will continue her happy life with her father. I felt that even if I may suffer some life-threatening illness because of going through IVF so many times, and going through all the stress and tension from IVF closure, at the end I will be blamed for my own illness. And if I end up sick, it will be caused by my inability to keep myself away from that stress and for not being able to make the decision to either stop fertility treatments, even with divorce as a consequence, or to conceive with the donor eggs.

As I said, the only thing that really kept me going was my daughter, and the only time that I felt anything close to happiness was when I was with her. But it was becoming hard for me to have the overwhelming feeling of a great extremely loving and caring mother, as I had during the first years of her life. At that time my husband accused me of being a bad mother in comparison with other mothers from our social circle, because of "my decision not to provide siblings to our child." And even the happy time spent with my daughter was greatly disturbed by all my worries, concerns, guilt, and fears about the future.

My enthusiasm for life, my optimism, and my energy all were destroyed. I was broken as a person, as a woman, as a mother, as a professional. None of my achievements meant anything to me anymore. My whole life was shattered, and I felt completely worthless. It was very hard to go through that difficult time totally alone, as I did not have close friends or relatives nearby.

My father lived in Europe and was always available to have long conversations with me over the phone, to advise me, to try to protect me and help me in this difficult situation. He acknowledged being "on my side" and how hurt he was by my husband's behavior and by the way my husband was treating me. My father was not advising me to divorce, but I felt that I would have his full emotional and financial support if I made that decision. My father's advises were: "Take good care of your health; Do not allow him to humiliate you; Reject guilt from your side in this situation and these circumstances; Stop fertility treatments and further ruining of your health; Try being less emotional; Don't have fears, since he is going to use them against you; Get advice from marital counselors; Collect information about the law; Care for the child in a natural and spontaneous manner, despite the threats he is imposing; Do not have false hope that he is going to change; Keep your job; Don't buy into his blackmail and bullying."

But I was careful how often I would call my father, as he was already in his seventies and with a heart failure. And during the worse time of my IVF closure crisis I planned to go to Europe with the child to spend vacation with my father, as soon as he recovers from his bypass surgery. I was full of hope that surgery will prolong his life, but unfortunately it took his life, suddenly and too early. I was devastated and every day of my life I feel that loss. I lost someone who loved me entirely and who was looking out for my interests and interests of my child. My father left me a heart full of his love, support and respect for who I am and what I achieved in life, and reminded me not to allow the destruction of my own life and future. He helped me to regain myself respect and self esteem, assured me that I wasn't a monster mother who selfishly decided not to get pregnant again (as I felt sometimes under my husband's accusations), but a hero mother who, with the enormous efforts tried to have more children, mostly for the sake of her child to have siblings. He encouraged me to believe in myself, to keep my values and to concentrate on what is good for my daughter and me. If he had lived longer, maybe I would have been brave enough to file for divorce and start a new life with his support.

Unfortunately, throughout the early years in North America, I had no time or interest in making close friends. My husband was my best and my only friend. Plus, working full-time, managing a household, having a small child, and going through IVF completely absorbed my time and making new contacts, friends, network was at the bottom of my priority list for years. Yes, we as a couple and family had our small social circle, but those were not friends I could turn to in a time of crisis. I believed that it would be shameful to badmouth my spouse in front of our mutual friends, not that much for my husband's reputation but even more for my. I recalled that whenever I heard public "spousal badmouthing" no matter that possibly spouse who was badmouthing was objectively right, somehow the whole situation made him or her sound as a "bad guy" and loose the respect from the mutual friends. Doing so, I would also put our friends in the uncomfortable situation to take a stand for one of us and mutual friends usually do not do that while couple is in conflict but still married. Before the divorce, friends' involvement is risky; if the couple at the end falls in love again and decides not to divorce, mutual friends would most probably feel awkward and that friendship will be sacrificed.

The fact that I had no one to talk in person, to vent, to ask for the opinion or advice, made my situation even hundred times worse. I had no choice than to write, as that was what I liked to do throughout my life. And usually the best inspiration for the artwork does not come from the state of happiness, but from pain, suffering and solitude. And I had all of these at that time and I wrote a theatre play and movie screenplay about the couple who could not have kids, whose love transformed into the hate. I also wrote in my diary when I needed to release my feeling. This helped to ease my great suffering, emotional pain, and feelings of guilt, which I can honestly describe as the greatest desperation and humiliation that I ever felt in my whole life. I felt it with such intensity and for such a long duration, and without any close person to share my emotions with, or seek the advice and help from. My diary became a friend of sorts, but a real friend would have been much better.

To Divorce or Not to Divorce

If there is conflict of interest between parents and children who share 50 percent of each other' genes, how much more severe must be the conflict between mates, who are not related to each other? All that they have in common is a 50 percent genetic shareholding in the same children. Since mother and father are both interested in the welfare of different halves of the same children, there may be some advantage for both of them in cooperating with each other in rearing those children. If one parent can get away with investing less than his or her fair share of costly resources in each child, however, he will be better off, since he will have more to spend on other children, by other sexual partners, and so propagate more of his genes.[1]

The more my husband pressured me, the more he tried to put all the responsibility and guilt toward our child on me, the more I rejected the idea of conceiving, bearing, and giving birth to a child that was genetically his, but not genetically mine. Eventually, it became completely unacceptable. And I had no desire, by having more children conceived through egg donation, to stop my husband from leaving me to find younger, fertile woman. He didn't miss any opportunity to cruelly remind me about this, as that was an option he would always have and could consider when the time came. The IVF science and industry gave him power over me, as his infertility was scientifically overcome by the implementation of ICSI, and he would most probably be successful in having kids with a more fertile woman, although she, too, would have to undergo IVF/ICSI. He used that power to bully me and blackmail me when I lost my reproductive potential. It was cruel and undeserved, in my opinion. If he had shown his cards, so to speak, in the earlier stages of our IVF battle, letting me know how long he would be willing to try with IVF and what his intentions and desires would be if we did not succeed with IVF, it would have been much better for him, for me, and for our child. I think we would have been able to go on living happy, possibly under some new arrangements, marriages, and families. If in the beginning of our struggle for children through IVF, when I possibly still hadn't lost my reproductive potential, my husband had told me clearly and honestly what his ultimate expectation of me was in the event that we failed with IVF, or even to get into some domestic contract agreement, I would have been able to find a way to compromise; our power in the situation would have been balanced, and he would not have able to bully me or issue ultimatums. Also, my own potential to have more biological kids with another man and create siblings and a family for my daughter would have inspired me and given me hope, enabling me to eventually make the decision to ask for a divorce. But by the time of IVF closure, there were no more opportunities for me to have more kids, so I couldn't create siblings for my daughter or start a new family. The best thing I could offer to my child was to preserve the family we already had, or at least to try not to destroy it. Not that I didn't have some hopes that I would find a man with whom I would fall in love and who would fit with my daughters' and my life, however through the time I realized that such a scenario, if not impossible, was very difficult, as I was not having male friends and admirers "in reserve", who could possibly exchange the role with my husband. My reality was that I had to start from the beginning in building network and friendships with the men and if I am lucky, after few years to succeed in finding another love of my life.

---

[1]   Richard Dawkins, *The Selfish Gene* (New York: Oxford University Press, 1989).

I chose to let my husband take responsibility for making the decision to get a divorce; I did not want to do him a favor by filing for divorce, as that was his initiative, not mine. I forced myself not to do it, because again my husband did not only make me responsible and guilty for failing to provide our daughter with siblings, but also wanted me to take a sole responsibility for failing to keep our family together. If I had more than one child, making the decision to divorce would have been much easier for me. I would not have been afraid to become a single parent, solely responsible for supporting, educating, and taking care of the kids. With at least two kids, in my mind, I would have a family, but having only one child, who would have to spend half of each week with each parent, was not even close to my vision of a family.

For a prolonged time, my husband and I tried to negotiate about the divorce. I was ready to sign an agreement for the divorce, as long as he agreed to leave our child with me as the primary parent. I said that he could see her on weekends and whatever other times we agreed upon, as long as she did not live with him. However, from our conversation about separation, it became obvious that our divorce would turn very nasty, involving lawyers, going to court, lots of money spent, and even more bitterness. I felt certain we would even end up hating each other. After even threatening that he would take our daughter from me, my husband's firm condition for separation was to have 40 percent shared custody of our child. My lawyer advised me that when spouses go to court, no matter what has happened between them, North American laws usually support shared custody, no matter how old the minor child is. If the parents cannot agree to any other scenario, the child may end up spending three and a half days a week in one parent's home, and three and a half days a week in the other parent's home. Also, in negotiations for separation, my husband was not willing to cover more than 50 percent of the huge financial debt caused by fertility treatments, leaving me with a 50 percent share of the debt, which would mean that I would probably not be out of debt for the rest of my life, despite the fact that through my employer medications for fertility treatments were to some extent covered and despite the fact that I was from day one of our marriage continuously working full time.

And at the top my husband wanted to get out of separation as a "good guy" and he tried to make me be a "bad guy". Of course what mattered to me most was our daughter and how divorce will affect her. I was a child from the divorced parents and although I could hardly remember life while my father was still in the family, I did miss his close presence in many aspects through the life. Again, my husband wanted to build his happy future on my expense. Recognizing that I started acting less emotional but more rational. My message was: you can leave me any time and you are more welcome to do it, but you are going to make that decision and live with the consequences of it, not make me do it for you, as you are the one who is unhappy with this family and you think that you deserved better. Only then we could both move on.

I would have accepted paying off half of the debt caused by fertility treatments, but I couldn't accept living without my child 50 percent of the time. The separation agreement, satisfactory for each of us and in our daughter's best interest, appeared entirely impossible to reach, and that pushed me even deeper into the nightmare. As I've said, I did not have any close friends or family in North America at that time; I had no support system, no one to help me or even just to listen to what I was going through. When I called a women's center, they advised me to take a child with me and come to the abused women's shelter; while living in the shelter, they told me I should file for the divorce. But although my husband was mean to me and treated me badly, he was still the father of my child; he was not a monster or a criminal, and I could not take our child and flee from our home. I wanted to behave like a civilized person and not to take some steps that might have helped me at that time, but that also could have backfired on my child in the present and the future.

With such a complicated separation scenario, I greatly envied women whose husbands agreed to leave home and see the kids once a week or even less often than that. I felt completely miserable and totally trapped by my life circumstances, as if I were in a labyrinth with no way out. In another way, it felt like my life was a house of cards that had suddenly collapsed. If I was caught in such a scenario but without a child, it would have not taken me long to divorce, but with the child, I felt instinctively that my primary responsibility was to build a support system and foundation for future life—for her sake. While living with continuous IVF, my career and income had stagnated for years. I did not invest in friendships, or any other personal fulfilments, as all my energy, time, and effort went into my marriage and family, as well as my coping with infertility. I wanted to build a successful future in different life aspects, both personal and professional, and I was convinced that if only I could succeed in that, I would also be able to make the decision to divorce with enough self-confidence and dignity to take my daughter with me and start a new life. I also wanted to be a role model for her, to bring her up with certain values, with self-respect and self-esteem, but for the first time, I hated my life, and I felt that I was a person without any value.

For a long time, I was at the edge of the desperation, and spending as much time as possible with my daughter saved me. I went alone with her everywhere, including vacations. My husband and I lived as a divorced couple for a long time, except that we all lived together in the same home. The only thing preserved, even in the time of escalated marital crisis, was to some extent the form and atmosphere of the family in front of our child, and I was happy for the fact that we were able to hide our marital problems in front of her. Around our daughter, we were still together, celebrating Christmas, Valentine's Day, Easter, and her birthday as a family.

I was going through an awakening, accepting reality and trying to invest in myself, listening to my inner voice. I expended great effort to regain my spiritual and physical balance and peace of mind in order to continue to function normally while trying to settle and resolve my problems. I accepted the situation, and I even understood that my husband had a right to do whatever he wanted, including finding another woman who would "provide" him with more kids. I wouldn't have a valid reason to hate him for that, only maybe for the way he went about it and the cruel words he used to express his feelings. He should have simply come to me, announced what he wanted, and then done it, not tried to force me to do something that I didn't want to, combined with belittling me, accusing me, and building my guilt toward our child. But I later realized that he couldn't do it the way I wished he would have, because he wasn't ready to take responsibility for such a decision. I also realized that he might have never wanted anything else than our family to be perfect.

It took me a long time to become less emotional about my husband's accusations and the pressure he put on me. It took me a long time to regain my self-esteem and self-respect, to recover from my disappointments, to enjoy my bond with my daughter without feeling any guilt about her lack of siblings, to build some real friendships, and to have some personal and professional achievements and successes. It also took a long time to fully understand my husband's nature, and to take responsibility for and live with the consequences of my own blind love for him and my decision to link my entire life with his. Most difficult of all, was being able to finally reject the guilt he had imposed on me, and to realize that most of these accusations were the voice of one frustrated, selfish, sadistic, and narcissistic man. This took the longest to accomplish, and I have not yet fully done so. I went to marital counselling alone; I invited him to go with me, but as I expected, he refused to come. He always knew exactly what he wanted in life, what he sought and strove for, and there was no one who could change his mind or give him advice. And even if he had made wrong choices and decisions in the past, he would never admit it. After a while, I stopped going to marital counselling because, without a spouse, it didn't make sense and wasn't even helpful.

I recalled that through all of our life together, my husband was results oriented but not too much concerned how he or we will achieve results. He tended to strive for perfection—or more precisely, the appearance of perfection. Whatever was not perfect was hidden between us. Also, he relied a lot on me to achieve those goals and objectives of perfection. And for him, many times perfectionism was having grass greener than the neighbor's. He could not be perfect, and we could not be a perfect family with just one child. My husband failed to realize that when someone forces another person to achieve perfection he first has to be a role model of attaining perfection. Not only to inspire, but also to take a great part in, and do the work associated with, achieving the goal of perfection. I felt deep inside that nobody, not even my husband, could force me to do what I didn't want to do, or at least what I was not able to do without great emotional, spiritual, and practical support. My husband had a great desire for a big family, but he did not have a passion for the idea of it. And the only person who had the passion to make that big family out of the impossible was supposed to be me. But instead of love, respect, tenderness, care, understanding, vision, and a fair share of family duties, he tried to build that passion in me out of fear and guilt. No passion ever comes from force and pressure.

I realized that I could not expect my husband to change; the only change I could create was within me: my perceptions, my attitude toward him, and my respect for myself. For a few years, I maintained an emotional distance from him. That distance protected me from further suffering and disappointments, and it helped me to love myself more, doing the best for myself in my personal interests, living my own life in accordance with my personal values, and being happy and true to myself. I knew that was the only way I could be the best mother for my daughter. Most of the time, I managed to remain undisturbed by his personality and actions, except when he imposed an unhealthy influence toward our daughter. I totally released him from any obligations and loyalty toward me and left him to live in complete freedom so that he could meet another woman and pursue his new life. I really hoped that would happen. I wanted it that way in order to be released for my new life, without any responsibility toward him or any guilt toward our daughter.

Dealing with the Guilt

It wasn't dealing with the emotional pain, disappointments, bullying, divorce, financial insecurity, losing social status, or loneliness that affected me the most. What struck me the most deeply during the time of IVF closure and the marital crisis that followed was the guilt that my husband foisted on me, and negative propaganda about me not being able to provide siblings to our child, attempting to drive a wedge between my child and me. But at the same time he was deliberate in building a good self-propaganda of a father whose priority objective is to have more children, the image that I hadn't ever ruined by telling our daughter that the reason for her to be the single child was actually her father's infertility.

I managed to some extent to understand my husband's desperation, and to forgive him for imposing pressure and a burden on me during the time of IVF closure, but I would never forgive him for trying to destroy my relationship with my daughter. He didn't hesitate to put a mother in conflict with her own child and to use that as a tool to achieve his objectives, all disguised as "being in the child's best interest." He never stopped expressing his belief that our child was greatly disabled because she was an only child, and he continually acted in accordance with that belief. Anything bad that happened to her (such as falling from the bike), or any inappropriate behavior from her (such as being very shy), was a consequence of her being an only child. According to him, being an only child would put her at a disadvantage in social environments and make her feel insecure and deprived of any support system or protection. He insisted that it would very negatively affect her life in every way. He also did not abstain from intentionally influencing our daughter and reinforcing her wishes for a sibling. It wasn't just once that she said to me, "Mama, why did all your babies die? And now I am alone." Or, "Mama, you are the meanest person in the world. You didn't give me any siblings."

I understood my husband's belief, and to a certain extent I agreed with his statement that mother was of less importance for our daughter than siblings, as I, her mother, am not going to live forever, but siblings would be with her all her life. That aspect had special importance because she would be a first-generation immigrant in North America, without any other family members. At the time of escalating crisis, I did not feel important to my child or essential to her future, and I greatly feared that death would come to take me for my child's sake.

The most difficult challenge for me was to reject the guilt that my husband kept imposing on me toward our daughter, and to try to live a happy life, ignoring his words and actions.

He, who was sterile and could not have kids in any other way than through IVF/ICSI was accusing me of the fact that our child did not have siblings! He was not taking one percent of the guilt on himself for not knowing true facts about his diagnosis at the beginning of our marriage. And then he was forcing separation in my age 43+, not while I was still fertility-wise younger when I would have been able to have more children naturally with a fertile man and our daughter would have had siblings. And finally he was not working on Plan B, but again expecting me to develop and work on an alternative plan for a big family.

I was ready to divorce rather than to spend the rest of my life punished with feelings of guilt toward my child. I was aware that the guilt imposed on me was something I would feel for the rest of my life. Because I did feel guilty, and I still do. Especially when I see my child very lonely or very bored, and I know that she is missing the company of other kids. And unfortunately, I could not close my eyes to the fact that we lived in an environment where families had average of 2.5 kids. And there were constant reminders, on a daily basis, that my child was an only child. In magazines, there were never pictures of happy smiling families with only one child; on TV commercials and programs, there are always big families. Many times, while my child was still little, I had to swallow the thoughtless comments some people would make, when they demanded more than asked, "Why are you waiting for so long for the second one? You'd better give your child a sibling!?" I knew that I didn't have to explain anything to anyone, and I didn't have to care what anyone thought or said. But in that vulnerable time of IVF closure and marital and family crisis, I was very hurt whenever anything reminded of the fact that my child would remain an only child, despite all the IVF efforts for so many years. It was the truth of those reminders that made me feel sad, not other people's opinions or comments. For the same reason, one question and remark from people will haunt me forever: "How many kids do you have? Just one?!?!" And even now at age forty-seven, while finishing this book, it still hurts me when people make such comments, followed by the question of why I don't have more kids. Based on all the false information the media spreads about women having babies at age fifty and even sixty, people still believe that having no more than one child is just a woman's sole decision or wish.

Forgiving but Not Forgetting; Family Reconciliation

> *Forgiveness in no way requires that you trust the one you forgive. But should he finally confess and repent, you will discover a miracle in your own heart that allows you to reach out and begin to build between you a bridge of reconciliation. And sometimes—and this may seem incomprehensible to you right now—that road may even take you to the miracle of fully restored trust.*

> —Wm. Paul Young, *The Shack*

Not that I was naive enough to have ever expected from my husband something that would not have been in keeping with his personality and his relationship with me, but I think that it would have been perfectly fair if my husband had come to me at the time of IVF closure and said, "Thank you for everything you did. I admire your strength, passion, energy, and persistence. I appreciate your sacrifice. I am thankful that you didn't leave me for another man who was fertile. I will never forget and I will always admire the fact that you not only accepted my infertility, which became a more painful part of your life than my own, and that you fought very hard, wasting your own health, time, energy, career, and other accomplishments. And thanks to you, we have this beautiful, smart, precious child: our beloved daughter."

And I would not have been surprised if he had come to me at the time of IVF closure and said, "Oh my dear, Anastasia! I would like to take you around the world! I would like to fulfill your wishes, your dreams. I would like you to get your life and well-being back. I would like to enjoy life together with you and the gift from God that we were blessed with, our daughter." I wouldn't have been much surprised because it would have fit the perception I had of our relationship, which, until that time, I was convinced was full of mutual love, care, and respect.

Now, feeling almost like someone analyzing my marital and family situation from a distance, I can say that there was a great misunderstanding between my husband and me, and a huge difference in feelings and emotional expectations, through all our years of undergoing IVF. Over the years my conviction, which happened to be based on the wrong assumption, was that my husband felt obliged to let me undergo IVF in order to compensate for my own desire to have more biological kids and a big family, as he, being infertile, wasn't able to have them naturally. Probably for all the years of IVF my husband did feel some subconscious guilt; however, from the time our child was born his guilt was not toward me but toward our daughter. And he found the sophisticated way to get away with his guilt by passing it on me. When we, after all the years of IVF, ended up not conceiving another child, he accused me of behaving selfishly toward our child, insisting that my decision not to have more children conceived through the donor eggs and to continue undergoing IVF only for my biological kids was going to ruin our daughter. My husband imposed very intelligent and cunning cruelty over the years by passing on to me, directly or indirectly, the hidden message: "Yes, my infertility is the why we could not have biological kids without IVF/ICSI, but with my initiative to have kids the other way (with donor eggs), I am overriding my deficiency and removing any guilt from my side. It is *your* decision not to go ahead with that plan, for which you should feel guilty for destroying our child's life and keeping her an only child, and a "handicapped" child and person, for the rest of her life."

At the end of IVF, my husband did not let me grieve. Going through IVF for years, I had ups and downs, and there were times I felt grief because I hadn't conceived; however, right up to the end, I always had hope that conquered my grief. It was probably different for my husband, who watched everything from a distance, more or less, not really being involved in the IVF protocols to anything close to the extent that I was. If he had understood and respected my need to grieve, let me grieve and helped me deal with it, I probably would not have suffered as much as I did, and we would most likely have come together to find a solution. But he wasn't there for me, and he didn't share my grief because he had nothing to grieve about: he was eager to have the kids he wanted by using donor eggs.

> *Grieving for an unborn child is complicated, as the loss is so intangible. It is a loss of possibilities. There is no body, no funeral, no ritual to mark this event. Others around you may not be sensitive to your loss or be unaware of what you are experiencing. Yet you may be experiencing a grief as profound as that of a parent whose child has died. You are not exaggerating or overreacting. Allow yourself to acknowledge just what it is that you have lost.*[2]

---

[2]   *Taking Charge of Your Infertility*, written by the Counselors at Melbourne IVF, edited by Kay Oke (Melbourne IVF, 1999)

After two years of marital crisis, I finally managed to forgive my husband to some extent, to stop hating him, and to regain some respect for him. I realized that one of the reasons I was not able to divorce him was that, deep in my soul, I knew that he did not have bad intentions. He didn't want to enjoy life as a bachelor, he wasn't a womanizer, and he was to a fair extent responsible for the family and our child. He just wanted a big family with many kids, and his objective was actually the same as mine. The only problem was his behavior and his attitude. He wanted things to happen, he wanted to "manage" and "direct," and again, he wanted to put all the load and activities to be on me. Even worse, he didn't show any gratitude and appreciation for my enormous efforts, and he did not offer a mature and responsible approach to resolving such a complex problem. It took me a while to realize that my husband's thinking, which was perfectly rational to him, was probably like this: if I'd already done so much, had the mental and physical energy and guts to persevere, ruined my physical health and well-being without succeeding to have another biological child, I should be willing to "going the extra mile" in order to create siblings for our daughter! I imagine that most, if not all, fertility doctors and other fertility clinic staff, if they ever read this, would agree with my husband's attitude. What my husband and clinics were failing to understand was that I wanted, with all my heart, (and I also had a right) to have more of my own biological children, not just any children with donors eggs. Wish for more of my own children, siblings for my daughter was the strong motivation which kept me going through the 7 years of IVF.

Our family slowly started to reconcile. Over time, my husband did not pursue starting a new family, although he threatened to do it many times. He showed signs of being glad to see me more relaxed and less stressed-out because of our situation. He showed some maturity and flexibility, and he indicated his wish to save our family. After a prolonged time, my husband finally backed off with his complaints about the size of our family, the impact of our child's being an only child and my responsibility for her lack of siblings. I tried not to keep dwelling on what had happened, and not to anticipate what would happen between my husband and me; instead, I tried to just live life.

At that time, we had many discussions about possible adoption. Again, my husband expected me to take the lead and to be passionate about it. But I could not have passion out of fear that things with the adoption might go wrong and that once something went wrong, my husband would be the first one to turn his back and find a way out of the situation—for himself, not me. And I was scared to death that if things did go wrong with the adoption, I would also risk losing my own child for 50 percent of the time. It could have easily happened that the adopted child did not fit in our family or that my husband's visions and expectations as to the adopted child's health, intelligence, or personality might not pan out, and then, instead of happiness and progress, it would just bring more stress and problems into our lives. I insisted on trying foster parenting first, and then if that worked, we could consider adoption. I wanted to have a test for all of us, to see how we would function with the foster child. But my husband was not open to that scenario. For him, that seemed a waste of time. He wanted a permanent child, not a temporary child. He accused me for seeing glass half empty rather than half full. And I admitted that I did, but after so many years of being very positive and strong in the extremely difficult life situation and at the end being betrayed by him, I could not allow myself taking any huge risks anymore.

I worked on myself a lot. I tried to convince myself that I should see so many good things in our family and marriage and that many women marry with less love, less mutual respect, and fewer values and good qualities in their relationships. I knew that in order for marriage to survive many years, apart from love and respect there shall be also a lot of compromising and tolerance and a motivation to preserve marriage. And I was to some extent motivated to preserve my marriage since I did not see other options acceptable for me, with some prospect for the new family. I, as a child of divorced parents was not a great fan of single parenting, especially with one child only. After two years of marital crisis, I tried to see only good things in our family life. I tried to imagine that the crisis had never existed and that we had just turned a new page in our lives. I tried to enjoy our family moments with our daughter the way I used to. I knew that if my husband and I had one thing in common, it was that we both truly loved our daughter and wanted all the best for her in this life. Although our ways and approaches were different, and during the marital and family crisis we had been in conflict, I knew that we were the two human beings on the planet who most loved our daughter. And despite the fact that I felt the lack of love, respect, care, and friendship from my husband which hurt me a lot, and that through the time I started to feel in a similar way towards him, it mattered more to me that he was the father of my daughter. Even if I had divorced him, I would have first looked for a good stepfather for my daughter than for a man with whom I would be passionately in love. I knew that I would only be able to love the man who would fit well with my daughter and me. Maybe I was just not lucky to meet the right guy yet.

My understanding of and feelings about our marriage began to evolve. I realized that it was a process and that it changed over time. Marriages that adjust to the changes and challenges of life will endure. Marriage is not necessarily just about mutual love and respect, although these are probably the two most important aspects of a good marriage. But beyond that, marriage is a way of life. And if we love our life—personal, marital, and family—we love our partner as well. Maybe it all starts from each partner's love for himself or herself. By that I mean healthy self-love, not narcissism. If partners express love, respect, and even admiration for who they really are, and then support and help each other to live the life they want to live, love grows and deepens between those partners, and they are able to maintain the love and the marriage for years and even decades.

Marriage and a family are also life investments. Now that I can look at our marital crisis from a distance, I realize that one of the major reasons I did not divorce my husband was my own reluctance to find myself in a position where I could lose everything, almost overnight, after so much investment in that marriage and family. More than just reluctant, I was angry. I kept thinking that I was now a middle-aged woman who had made an enormous investment in many ways. I had invested my health, my time, my career, my money, my energy, and my love, and even after all these investments, I still faced losing not only the love of one man (God save me from such a love), my husband, along with my social status, marriage, and family, but also, and most important of all, the primary custody of my child! And I felt bitter and angry that because of such a bad investment, I had lost my reproductive potential and my potential children who now would never be born. For all the years that I'd invested in IVF in order to have more children with my infertile husband, by losing my reproductive potential, I also lost value "on the market," so to speak—not every market, but the one market that I was interested in! Not that I wasn't an attractive woman and that I wouldn't be able to find a man, but to find the man who would be good to my daughter, whom I would be able to love and fulfill my life's dreams with. But I wanted a family and kids, and for me, that scenario was already over. It would be very difficult for me to find a divorced man or widower with kids around my own child's age. The best that I could expect would be a divorced baby boomer a bit older than I, with kids already in college, who would be happy to have a younger, good-looking woman, full of energy and established in her own career, even if it would mean being a stepfather to her child. But I wasn't too excited with the vision of life with such a man, even if he was crazy in love with me and very good to me, with whom I could go on the fantastic trips, have adventures, have a rich social and cultural life, feel as a beautiful woman and respected intellectual and so on. Because my life was still in playgrounds, parks, waterparks, beaches, sand castles, birthday parties, play dates, play time, after school activities, farms, campgrounds, fairs, circus, IMAX cartoons, toys, board games etc. and I felt that only man who has a similar life style with his kids (similar age like my daughter) would fit in for love and relationship with me. I also had my doubts about how much more I would be willing to invest in a new relationship, to start from scratch in my mid-forties, when I was already totally exhausted and wanted every moment of my free time to spend with my child and to have finally some personal time that I did not have for more than ten years.

It is possible that my husband also thought of our marriage and family as an investment of his time, effort, money, etc. He had no reason to be bitter about having invested so much; his bitterness came from the fact that he ended up being the father of only one child. Maybe he was reluctant to give up the marriage and family where he had to invest so little because he was aware that he would have to invest much more of himself and his time, energy and money in a new family with newborns and with the wife not as much contributing to the family as I did. It would have been quite easy for him to find a much younger woman who would agree to go through IVF, but most probably he would have been limited to women who were not financially independent and possibly not on his intellectual level, which could have been one of the compromises that he was possibly not willing to make.

It could also have been that the reason we did not divorce was that both my husband and I had a strong sense of "the third force in the room," as described in the book *The Good Marriage—How and Why Love Lasts,* by family psychologist Dr. Judith S. Wallerstein and *New Your Times* science writer Sandra Blakeslee. During the 1990s, they studied fifty successful marriages and observed that, in virtually every case, the partners treated their union like a precious, separate entity deserving respect and nurture. In good marriages, the authors concluded, both partners treasure their collective identity more than their individuality:

> *It looks as if both partners love each other as individuals—but they love their love even more. They exalt it. They celebrate it. They talk about it as if it is the third force in the room, created by their merged commitment. They revere it and routinely and willingly make sacrifices for it.*[3]

Maybe, despite all that happened, I still loved my husband. Isn't love blind, at least to some extent blind? I liked having a partnership with him, I liked caring for him, and I liked the life we had. For many of our years together, we were very compatible, we had a way of life for each of us individually and together that we both enjoyed and were comfortable with. The irony was that my love for him was reinforced through the years of IVF. Without a feeling that our destiny was to be together "until death do us part," I probably would not have been able to stay with an infertile man and go through all the hardships of IVF. And what kept me willing to stay with him, even during the times when I felt that I preferred never to see him again, was that he was the father of my beloved child, our beloved child, and that we had once lived as a very happy family. Deep inside me, maybe I just wanted that time to come back again.

I finally felt that I could forgive my husband, but I knew that I would not be able to forget and trust him—ever. And to this day, I don't know if he forgave me, or if he ever will.

---

[3]   Judith Wallerstein and Sandra Blakeslee, *The Good Marriage—How and Why Love Lasts* (New York: Warner Books, 1995).

EPILOGUE

When you look at the moon, you think, "I'm really small. What are my problems?" It sets things into perspective. We should all look at the moon a bit more often.

—Alain de Botton

More than anything in the world, I wished to finish this testimony with the story of how my second baby was finally born. For a long time, I was not ready to say that it would never happen—or to believe that it would never happen. I kept hoping that a miraculous invention in ART science might occur before my reproductive age was completely over. I hoped for a natural miracle; I hoped that I would experience a moment of epiphany, deciding to become pregnant with donor eggs and discovering that there was no difference between loving my own biological genetic child and one that was mine biologically but not genetically. And yet, despite all that hope, my second baby will never be born.

I learned many life lessons from this experience, all of which I would be much happier to never have learned, to never have needed to learn. Maybe I became a bitter and cynical person, or perhaps I become what some people might describe as mature and less naive. This life experience might not have made me a better person; however, I hope it made me take better care of myself, fulfill some of my dreams, and stop relying on anything or anyone. But after going through this experience, I feel very lonely in this world.

Yes, it is true what Friedrich Nietzsche said that "what does not destroys you makes you stronger," but there are many details missing from that statement. It is not that what doesn't kill person just makes him or her stronger, it is also that what doesn't destroy a person makes him or her tougher, more selfish, more aggressive, more unhappy, more vulnerable, more disappointed, more realistic, more envious, more competitive, more cunning, more sarcastic, more frustrated, more tired—the list goes on and on. What doesn't destroy a person also makes him or her less loving, less caring, less understanding, less patient, less tolerant, less optimistic, less naive, less trustworthy, less loyal—and that list goes on and on too. After all that happened to me while going through IVF, and especially during IVF closure, I felt like I would never again be a nice and quiet person who just minded her own business and trusted the good in others. That was the way I was before IVF. Now I felt that deep inside I would always feel alone and vulnerable and that in order to protect myself and my future, and most important of all, my child and her future, I would have to be very smart, shrewd, practical, and proactive, always keeping in mind our best interests and the results I wanted for us.

I might have become stronger because of all that I went through, but if that is true, my strength is now based on trying to be less emotional and more practical. But the whole point of it is that I didn't want to have to be strong. I had been strong throughout enough of my life already, even before IVF: living in poverty during the communist regime and in post communist years, through the time of the failure of the Soviet Union, living through the first stressful years of immigration to North America, where we were poor once again and then had to struggle with infertility. As Mother Theresa said: "I know God will not give me anything I cannot handle. I just wish he didn't trust me so much."

So all I wanted was to finally live a nice and calm life, to enjoy every day and every minute with my daughter and my family. And to fulfill some of my dreams, other than having more children, to learn more things, to develop career, to get into the life some of my great ideas and creativeness, to travel, to read great books, to meet great people. And maybe, finally, at this stage of my life, I even deserved to start treating myself better. And I needed a strong shoulder to rest my head on. I wanted to have a responsible and mature man by my side. And I am not sure if my husband will ever again have that role in my life. My understanding of my marriage now is different from what I believed in when I got married and throughout the first happy years of my marriage. There was a permanent damage to my husband's and my relationship, to our friendship, trust, respect, loyalty etc. which with every day of marital crisis through the IVF closure turned to be more unrecoverable. Now I feel that it is a partnership of raising a child in a fairly good family environment.

For the rest of my life, I will be paying off the financial debt incurred by IVF. But that is not even comparable to the price I must pay in my heart for sacrificing my potential biological kids for a man who probably wasn't worth it. The absurd part of all this is that, if our IVF attempts to have more children hadn't failed, I probably never would have seen my husband's dark side, and then I never would have felt that he wasn't worth my love and sacrifice.

I always try to keep in mind that it could have been worse. During that brief moment, when our tiny embryo consisting of just a few microscopic cells began to divide in the laboratory, I know that God was on my side. And I hope that He still is.

Now, when I am finishing this book, I feel overwhelmed with happiness and self-respect because I succeeded in preserving my marriage and keeping my family together. The decision to divorce is not easy, but the decision not to divorce may be even more difficult. I hope that my child will be the one to benefit the most from my decision not to divorce.

I knew that I needed some solitude, and so I went alone on a Kilimanjaro climb. For a few days, I was surrounded only by nature, rocks, and sky. With every passing day, climbing ever higher, the air became thinner and harder to breathe. I found it difficult to manage the most basic human needs and functions: to breathe, to drink, to walk. Finally, when I got to the mountain summit, I was overwhelmed. One profound thought struck me, and I couldn't let go: Our lives, our happiness, our miseries, our joys, and our problems all look so small and insignificant when we stand on a mountaintop. That vantage point gives us perspective. It helps to remember how much we love life, especially when we face our fear of losing it. Spending time in Africa, the continent closest to Mother Nature, the continent that most resembles how our planet was during the time of humankind's early ancestors, I felt all the time surrounded by and assimilated into nature. I was aware that I was a part of it at every moment. I realized that nature cannot be confronted by me or anyone else. Only by staying in balance with it and accepting its rules can we bring ourselves closer to happiness.

And I feel much happier now than I did at the time of IVF closure, when our marital and family crisis began to escalate. I am finally ready to start enjoying life again after all those years of living a nightmare, and it appears that my husband, if not joining me, at least is not stopping me. Now I know that I am a special person, woman, and mother.

Through the time, strong bond with my daughter helped me to find my inner being again. My daughter and her friends became my best and almost the only company. I greatly enjoy watching kids being truly happy, discovering beauties and difficulties of life, growing and maturing. My happiest moments today are when I am making children happy. And being surrounded by children's purity, honesty, open heart, naivety, innocence, lack of hypocrisy, curiosity, cheerfulness, and positive energy, I am travelling though the time back to my youth, my soul is transforming to a soul of a child that I once was and I am slowly turning to the person I used to be - an open, spontaneous person, full of life joy and optimism. My feelings of guilt towards my daughter almost faded away, as I was seeing that she, with her caring, honest and tolerant personality already had a great ability to make friends. And I could only hope, that instead of people taking advantage of her loneliness, she will always have many good friends that she can rely on, who will compensate her for not having siblings and not having parents one day.

Am I happy now? Did I regain love for my husband? Did I forgive and forget? Am I ready to live happily ever after?

Yes. Every day of this short life. With my only child.

Author's photos at Mount Kilimanjaro summit

Letter to My Daughter

I want to devote the last paragraph of this testimony to my daughter. I don't want her to read this book. I just want her to get the message that I will send her throughout her life. I want her to be aware, not of my IVF struggle, but of the fact that she may be in risk for having the same challenge in her life, and that she should do everything possible to avoid it. She might have some genetic predisposition for infertility, although my understanding is that daughter of an infertile man is not affected by her father's infertility, since she received from him X chromosome, instead of the Y chromosome which carries the genetic defect. Even if perfectly fertile, she may easily end up delaying her motherhood, as women in today's Western society tend to do. I want to make sure that she undergoes all the necessary checkups for fertility potential as soon as she can, so that she will be aware of any potential diagnosis of eggs premature aging, or any other infertility diagnosis, early enough to address it. If necessary, I would encourage her to freeze her eggs while she is still young, fertility-wise. My objective in her upbringing from the very early years was to make sure that she would not get trapped in delayed motherhood, and thus, be at greater risk of needing to undergo IVF in order to have biological children. And I will warn her never to marry an infertile man, as there would not be a single man in the world worth giving her love to, if it meant the risk of sacrificing being able to have her own children.

Here is my letter to my daughter:

My darling,

From my early childhood, I imagined you and I loved you, through all the years that you did not yet exist. I always knew that you would be born one day.

Unfortunately, your wish for a baby sister or brother will never come true. Despite all the pennies thrown into fountains, all the prayers to God, and all the letters to Santa. And despite your mom going through IVF for so many years. I am so sorry for having you as an only child, something that you never wanted, that you never chose to be. I am sorry for my weakness, but I had to say "no" one day. No more fertility treatments, no more false hopes. I wanted to return to you, to be devoted to you, and to stop being so stressed by IVF, both physically and emotionally. I wanted you to have a healthy mother for as long as possible. I will try to replace your sibling and be your best friend.

I will not tell you that the most important things for women are education, career, independence, freedom, and achievement of dreams and ambitions. These are all important, but women can achieve all these things in today's world without too many obstacles. There is a bigger problem for women in today's world: finding a proper partner and future father for their kids, and finding him at the right time. That can be achieved only if you, while you are a young woman pursuing your goals in education, independence, and career, never lose sight of your personal and emotional life and always balance it through the years. If you concentrate too much on achieving the former, you may easily waste valuable time needed to achieve the latter. Extended time for a family and kids is not a luxury that women have, not even with the modern assisted reproductive technologies. If in your future, you balance your life ambitions with the role of a woman that nature gave you, nature will be on your side.

Be careful, and don't make the same mistakes I did! Don't delay your motherhood! Older you are riskier is if you will be able to have kids. Learn from my experience, and avoid getting into the same nightmare, which may not even end happily, as mine did because I had you. Throughout my life, I was optimistic and happy. I had many interests and dreams, and I always had a lot of energy and the passion to fulfill them. But coping with infertility ruined me and changed my spirit. I would not ever want you to go through any similar life difficulty.

Having kids is the most wonderful thing in life. Being a mother is the best experience that a woman can have. By having you, I discovered a whole new universe. Before you were born, I didn't know that having a baby in my lap would feel like an overwhelming happiness and reunion with the nature and eternity. Every day from the day you were born, I've felt like flying, happy and pleased to open eyes in the morning, to live another day with you. And I regret for not having you earlier to have more years of our lives spent in this world together!

I wish you all the best in life.

Yours,
Mom

(Written in the town where you were born, on your tenth birthday, July 2013)

PART II

CONCLUSIONS AND ADVICE

LESSONS I LEARNED

Our life is not determined by what happens to us, but by how we react to what happens; not by what life brings to us, but by the attitude we bring to life. A positive attitude causes the chain of reaction of positive thoughts, events, and outcomes. It is catalyst . . . a spark that creates extraordinary results.

—Steve Nakamoto

The Importance of Plan B and IVF Counseling

While going through the infertility battle, even in the very early stages, there should always be a Plan B. I think it is even helpful to apply that rule to all aspects of our future, as I learned a hard lesson because of having no Plan B for either my family life or my personal life during my struggle with infertility. I know now that even if the failure of our fertility struggle could not have been prevented, it would not have had such a tremendous impact on our life if we'd had a Plan B.

What is so hard about having a Plan B in infertility battles? It seems a simple question, but it does not have a simple answer. Truthfully, it should not be that hard from a practical standpoint; it should not be even too time-consuming, or expensive, as compared to the time and money spent and wasted on fertility treatments. Some extra time and effort could easily be spent surfing the Internet, researching different options through ART and/or adoption. The practical part is not what's hard. The hard part is of an emotional and spiritual nature. In order to have a Plan B in place, the couple has to be ready to accept the cruel reality that, despite all the effort, energy, hard work, tons of money, and enormous amount of time spent—or, they may feel, wasted—and possibly the temporarily or even permanently ruined state of the woman's health, there is a high probability that at the end they might not be blessed with a child. But that same couple undergoing IVF has to simultaneously be full of not just hope, but even passion, in order to be able to overcome the problems and cope with the challenges. And it is very difficult to manage so many conflicting emotions along with rational thinking. It is difficult, if not impossible, to be filled with hope while simultaneously accepting a painful reality. One solution might be for the couple to start working on a parallel plan while there is still hope. If Plan B is already in process, it is possible that the time when all hope finally has to be buried might coincide with the time of child adoption or any other option that the couple might have decided to go with as their Plan B. That would probably be the scenario that might spare the couple from enormous suffering, marital crisis, and even divorce, because it might help them to move on, almost immediately.

I believe that each IVF clinic should establish mandatory counseling for couples and that the counselor's role should be taken very seriously and even considered to be a crucial part of the entire IVF program. Counselors could help couples to choose an option for Plan B, and then to proceed with it, and this would help prevent marital crisis situations, such as one partner bullying the other, emotional blackmail, and so forth. The counselor's role should be to protect the interests of the woman, the man, the couple, and possibly even their born and unborn children. Counselors should also help each person to understand his or her partner's feelings, attitudes, expectations, and cultural and religious backgrounds, and finally, they should act as moderators and advisors. Mandatory IVF counseling, at least to some extent, could help each couple navigate the difficult time in life when they are going through infertility, and minimize the painful challenges and problems that arise when each couple is forced to choose childlessness, other ways to have children together, or separation.

Age, Age, and Nothing but Age

It would be dishonest to say that I do not regret considering having children earlier in life. Also, I regret for not being aware about the drastic decline of female fertility after the certain age. While going through the IVF I learned that the age when female fertility drops is not mid-forties but mid-thirties. I also learned that cut off age does not apply only to women who are already having fertility issues, but to the average healthy and fertile woman. And finally I learned the tough fact that assisted reproductive technology (ART) can do a very little to improve and overcome female biological clock.

I want to emphasize the importance of a woman's biological clock and patient awareness of it. I would suggest that the couple/woman tackle fertility issues on a full-time basis, just as soon as they discover that they might be infertile. Couples, especially the woman of the couple, need to be aware that the time of fertility flies and that no woman has the luxury of wasting it. If a woman has just hit her thirties, and for more than one or two years has been unable to conceive (provided that she has monitored her ovulation and made sure to have intercourse on her most-fertile days), I would suggest doing a complete fertility investigation on both partners. If the results show a problem—or if a problem clearly exists, but there is no explanation or diagnosis associated with it (unexplained infertility)—I would suggest going with the most invasive ART methods. With methods like IVF, there will be a high probability of success when the woman is younger and expected to respond well to the IVF hormonal stimulation. Younger women undergoing IVF may have a reasonable expectation, after one or two treatments, to have one child, or even twins, and also to have a number of frozen eggs.

Each case is different, of course, and the success of IVF does not depend only on the female patient's age. However, my understanding is that for the female patient aged thirty to thirty-five, it wouldn't be unreasonable to expect that IVF would result in ten to fifteen embryos ready for transfer. With only one IVF attempt, that woman will have the same chances to get pregnant as the same woman will have with five to ten IVF trials when she is thirty-eight to forty-two, if she produces only two embryos per protocol. Actually, her chances for successful IVF treatment when she is younger are even higher, because a younger woman's eggs are likely healthier, with good genetic material, and the probability of successful implantation is also higher. I am under the impression that even women who have a specific infertility diagnosis that prevents them from conceiving naturally, but who are still young, will have a much better chance of conceiving through IVF than women who have been fertile and healthy for their entire lives, but whose age has caused their fertility potential to decline and brought them close to the end of their reproductive time. My understanding is that a woman who is not regularly ovulating, or a woman who has polycystic ovarian syndrome or a disorder of the uterine lining, but who is still under thirty-five, has a much higher chance of conceiving through IVF than a woman over forty with elevated FSH and genetically older eggs.

My opinion is that it is not prudent to waste time on a special diet, taking vitamins, or doing IUI and similar ART methods, only to wake up one day at an age close to forty and with greatly decreased fertility, but with no baby. I don't think that infertile couples should rely too much on nonaggressive methods for a long time, especially when the woman is already thirty-five (or older), because from the age of thirty-five, the average woman's fertility drops with geometric progression. Nowadays, many women have a huge misconception, the same one that I had before I got into the fertility struggle and even during my first few years in IVF: that IVF can miraculously beat the biological clock. That happens only if a woman is extremely lucky, or extremely fertile at an older age, which depends on her natural, genetic fertility potential and can only be slightly enhanced with IVF. If a woman is perfectly healthy in terms of her reproductive system and fertility, and if she has average fertility potential relative to her age, my understanding is that her chances to conceive at an older age, even with IVF, would be very slim.

Similar to my case, there is already a generation of women (and a new one now coming of age) who were perfectly fertile and healthy up until that certain age, but who will, by making the decision or being forced by various circumstances to have children later in life, not have the opportunity to have children until close to, or even after the age of forty, and those women will inevitably face the painful reality that they have already missed the fertile reproductive age and be probably shocked by that discovery. If they still want to have children, they will then have to decide to adopt, to have a surrogate baby, to conceive through an IVF egg-donation protocol, or to stay childless.

In my opinion there are different reasons why women nowadays are having kids later, or even worse—too late to have kids. One reason is a very bad economy in many areas in the world, where people live in poverty and man of one generation are not ready to support families before age of 35 and later. The cruel reality is that a majority of the women of the same generation either marries man of the same age, but when they are older, with their fertility already declined, or stays unmarried and without kids, while these men marry younger women and make families. In western world again there are economic factors, but not as much based on poverty as on general need and greed for establishing social status and career before starting a family. I hope that my message throughout the book is very clear that there is no economic reason that is worth decision to delay having babies and even living very poor will not make person more miserable than later inability to have kids. The other reason in modern societies is that after the age of thirty for both man and women is becoming more difficult to find the partner. Because of the busy life style even young people who are still single are not having too many opportunities to meet possible future partner. I would suggest for women especially, before they hit very risky fertility-wise age, to allocate some active time for looking for partner. They may go on social and dating events, network with people, be open for new friendships etc. By only going to work and retuning home it is difficult, almost impossible, to meet a future partner. Finding a partner in any age is a full time job, but especially becomes difficult when there is less man on the market, which definitely starts in early thirties. And in the countries like Russia it is additionally challenging because the human sex ratio is 9 men to 10 women. And Russian human sex ratio might be one of the worse, however there are more women than man in all North America, all of the Europe (except for Albania and Macedonia), most of the ex Soviet Union countries, North Korea and Japan, south east Asia and Australia; most of the South America (except for Venezuela, Peru and Central America) and in half of the African continent.

Freeze and Thaw with IVF Statistics and Clinic Disclaimers

What frequently annoyed me during our journey through infertility was that we were part of one statistic one day, and another statistic the next day. This was very frustrating, to say the least!

The first time a fertility doctor rejected me for treatment with my own eggs, it was only five minutes after explaining that the probability of successful IVF with my own eggs was very low, that she asked me if I took folic acid daily. I couldn't believe what I'd just heard! Why would it matter if I took folic acid at all, if my chances for getting pregnant with IVF were close to zero, and it would be impossible for us to conceive naturally because of the male infertility factor? Maybe this doctor said that to cover herself in case I became pregnant miraculously, which would mean that even she was not 100 percent sure that my chances for conceiving were zero?

In another clinic, the doctor was not too optimistic about the positive outcome of an IVF/ICSI protocol; the odds were poor because I was already forty-two at the time. Despite my history as a low responder, the doctor insisted that we should sign a waiver stating that in the case of having three embryos transferred and successfully implanted, one of the three must be destroyed. We laughed while signing the document because, at that time, after almost five years of IVF/ICSI treatments, we never had more than two embryos transferred in a single protocol, and of the total of about fifteen embryos that we had transferred during those five years, only one had ever implanted!

I could easily imagine how a couple not very experienced with IVF might react when asked to sign such an agreement. Wouldn't they be under the wrong impression that they did not have to worry about anything other than avoiding a multiple pregnancy, when the real concern for most couples, even at the very beginning, should be whether they would ever have even one baby?

I understand that doctors have to give all these statistics and disclaimers in order to cover themselves for all possible liability circumstances. But what annoys me is that such a careless approach to legal liabilities results in presenting contradictory information and statistics to patients. That may cause patients to misinterpret medical facts, have incorrect perceptions and/or misconceptions, develop false hope, or conversely, it might destroy patients' hope and strength to continue, and even influence them to give up before all their chances are truly lost.

An Inconvenient Truth about Donor Eggs

I accept a good share of responsibility for being in this fertility nightmare, but if I had not been misled by the media, I would have been alarmed sooner, and then I might not have made certain mistakes. If I hadn't been fooled by false information and an unrealistic attitude toward female fertility, I would have possibly chosen a different path and made different decisions.

Over the years, there were many stories in magazines about older, and even very old, women having babies. In 2005, a woman in Romania, then sixty-six years old, got pregnant and gave birth to a healthy baby. And in 2007, a woman in Spain, then sixty-seven years old, gave birth to twins. Just go on Google and type into the search box something like "women over fifty having babies," and the following results will appear:

> *With the help of modern fertility treatment, many elderly women become pregnant.*

> *The number of women "cheating nature" to have babies well into old age will become even more common, and may herald the era of the seventy-year-old new mother, a fertility expert said.*

> *Doctor X said, "In my opinion, in the next five years, while we might not see hundreds of women aged sixty-plus become mothers, we will see an increase in their numbers."*

> *Obsessed with the desire to have a child, a seventy-year-old woman risked her life to go in for in vitro fertilization, a process by which eggs are fertilized by sperm outside the woman's womb. She gave birth to twins.*

And there are also stories about celebrities over forty who try to have baby with the help of ART. Usually, the first article is about seeing the celebrity couple in a fertility clinic, or the female celebrity alone if she is using donor sperm. Shortly after the initial story, the cover of the same magazine will feature a photo of the same female celebrity, with an arrow pointing to her "baby bump," as the media suspects that she is already pregnant! A few months later, the magazine announces the big news that the celebrity is pregnant. After the birth of the baby (or babies), the magazine has a special issue with numerous photos of the happy celebrity mother/couple with baby(babies), nursery, strollers, toys, and so on. The celebrity mother does not looking tired and fat; in fact, she looks better than ever, radiantly happy and with a perfect figure. Sometimes there is a more detailed story about the celebrity couple/woman coping with infertility and how they/she finally succeeded in having a baby. Regardless, most of these articles leave the reader with the false impression that as soon as someone decides to go to a fertility clinic, as long as he or she has enough money to undergo IVF, the very next step is the birth of a healthy baby, and often, more than one baby.

Over the years, I was one of the millions of women who read these articles and heard through the media about the miraculous scientific success of modern fertility treatments. I did believe that today's science could do almost anything in the sphere of infertility. With all these stories about women aged forty-five and even older having babies, who wouldn't believe that science couldn't accomplish miracles?

Magazine articles and the media fail to mention just one "minor" detail: that the majority of these postmenopausal women, and even premenopausal women, conceived their babies through an IVF donor-egg protocol. Of course, not all the older celebrity and noncelebrity mothers who underwent IVF had their babies through donor-egg protocols, and even if they did, they had a right to keep that information from the public and to protect their privacy. Nevertheless, in general, the media makes it seem like IVF will allow women or any age to become pregnant and deliver healthy babies.

Wikipedia, however, does give some information that is accurate to a certain extent, although it specifies women's age as "over 50," which is not true, because the information regarding fertility potential applies to a much younger age:

> *Pregnancy over age fifty has become more possible for women, due to recent advances in assisted reproductive technology, such as egg donation. Typically, a woman's fecundity ends with menopause, which by definition is twelve consecutive months without having had a period. Perimenopause usually begins between ages forty and fifty-one. This is when the periods become irregular and eventually stop altogether (men, in contrast, generally remain fertile throughout their lives, although the risk of genetic defects is greatly increased due to the paternal age effect). Pregnancy over age forty is associated with increased risks.*

(http://en.wikipedia.org/wiki/Pregnancy_over_age_50)

Not once I heard from women over 40 and even over 45 that they were regularly using contraception. And who could even expect that the average woman in today's society would know the truth about the female fertility and limits of IVF science when doctors, other than fertility specialists, gynecologists, and obstetricians, don't even know! The following is an actual conversation that I had with one physician:

ME: "Doctor, did you ever have a case when a woman of my age (forty-five) got pregnant?"

DOCTOR: "Sometimes."

ME: "Did they take some hormonal therapy in order for that to happen?"

DOCTOR: "You mean hormone replacement therapy? No."

ME: "No, I meant hormones to enhance their chances to conceive."

DOCTOR: "Not that I know of. As long as woman is having periods and ovulating normally, she can still get pregnant."

Unbelievable! That doctor was not even aware of the real facts about the average woman's fertility potential! As all my life before and even at that age, I still had regular periods, I ovulated promptly, and I didn't have endometriosis or similar conditions, but I learned from going through IVF that at the age of forty-one, my eggs were most probably already old and that it would be almost 100 percent impossible not only for me, but for most of the women at the age of forty-five, to conceive a child!

Unfortunately, the misconceptions and incorrect information provided by the media, or other authors, and even doctors and practitioners, who are either not well-informed or hiding the truth about the real capabilities, limitations, and success rates of ART procedures, have created and widely disseminated false perceptions about ART and IVF. And women who are misinformed and misled will pay the price. Plus, it is not only the women coping with infertility currently, but the huge population of women who will have to struggle with infertility in the future. The number of women and couples negatively affected by the media's misleading information will rise exponentially in the future, because women are getting married later and having kids much older than they ever did before. I strongly believe that it is of high importance to properly inform the female population about the true facts. It would also be of high importance to minimize the number of women misinformed about IVF capabilities, especially women already past thirty-five. There is already an ever-growing population of women suffering greatly when they face the truth that, although they can still have children through IVF in their late thirties and early forties, or even older, they will only be able to do so by with egg donation.

Clinics are very emotionless and practical when it comes to suggesting a donor-egg protocol. In my opinion, it is usually just going "by the book" when one of the following factors, or a combination of them, arises:

- The third IVF protocol fails.
- The woman's age is already advanced.
- The woman's FSH level is higher than 15.
- The clinic wants to get rid of the patient because of probable IVF failures in the future which will be diminishing clinics statistics or even involve the risk of a lawsuit.

Previously in this book, I talked a lot about the first three factors listed above, and their influence on the clinic's suggesting a donor-egg protocol. The last factor is based on my assumption that probably, with an increased number of IVF failures for the same woman/couple, the risk of a lawsuit is higher for that clinic. By declaring that clinic doesn't want to do more cycles with a woman's natural eggs, and by suggesting a donor-egg protocol as an option, the clinic minimizes its liability for continuing to receive payments of a significant amount from a woman/couple who has a very low probability of success. Not all clinics and clinic staff took that approach with me, and I was happy to be in a few clinics that wanted to deal with me as a patient with her own eggs, despite my fertility diagnosis and advanced age.

For the same couple who falls under the above category, most clinics will probably suggest going ahead with a donor-egg protocol. That scenario might not only be in the couple's best interest, but also in the clinic's best interest. Donor-egg protocols are much more successful than regular IVF for women with certain fertility problems and/or of a certain age. Donor-egg protocols do not ruin clinic statistics, whereas IVF treatments with a woman's own eggs, once she is older, do ruin those statistics.

Without established regulations for statistics on IVF success rates, it is very difficult to know what the real clinic success rates are, and clinics have a lot of freedom in deciding what statistics to disclose. The most telling factor would be if the clinic counts donor-egg pregnancies as part of the same statistics as all other pregnancies, as that number could easily lead to a greatly inflated—and thereby false—impression of that clinic's IVF success rates. I never looked at clinic statistics when choosing a clinic; I went with my overall impression, looking at the doctor's experience and/or my faith in whoever had referred me to that clinic. Also, in my final IVF years, Internet blogging about the clinics and doctors was already in place, and I had a chance to read other patients' comments.

MY RECOMMENDATIONS AND ADVICE
TO COUPLES AND WOMEN
UNDERGOING IVF

This chapter will provide my recommendations and advice to couples and women, based on my experiences, the lessons I learned, and the opinions and conclusions I formed as a result. As with the rest of this book, these opinions and conclusions are entirely my own.

Life during All-Consuming IVF

I suggest that from the first day of fertility treatments, the couple takes their IVF treatments very seriously and considers them a top priority. Even if everything goes smoothly and the treatment protocols are not too time-consuming, I would recommend not planning any activities other than ordinary daily ones during the time of the IVF treatments, which may last from two to six weeks, depending on the type of protocol. I also recommend not scheduling any vacations or long trips; not hosting any social events or parties at home; and not doing any home renovations or major housecleaning. My advice is to only engage in regular, routine, day-to-day activities, because the IVF struggle, over the time, may become very time-consuming and energy-depleting. Couples undergoing IVF have to be very focused, mentally and physically, on the solution of the infertility problem. They are living with continuous stress. They have to spend endless hours investigating a problem, trying to make the right decisions, going through the protocols, and keeping their bodies and spirits in good health. They have to console and support each other. Such couples also have to stay motivated and focused at work, striving for promotions or even getting new or second jobs, because they can't possibly foresee how much money they will have to spend in order to have a child—far more than couples without fertility problems, who don't spend very much money at all in order to get pregnant. (Of course, once the baby is born, it's a different story!) Couples struggling with infertility also need a lot of emotional strength. They must expect that people will talk about babies and kids all the time, which is very difficult when trying to cope with infertility, and couples in IVF should avoid being in company of these people. (Often, couples choose to keep their IVF private, as my husband and I did, so this chatter about babies and kids from others isn't necessarily unkind or uncaring, but it is painful and upsetting nonetheless.) Couples battling infertility should not feel bad if they sometimes seem to behave selfishly and neglect other people and their needs. They must remember that undergoing IVF is a very serious problem, and they do not have to feel obligated to sacrifice their energy, time, emotions or well-being in order to help others, especially those who just take and do not reciprocate with help, support, or kindness.

It is especially important for woman who is trying to get pregnant with IVF to keep her body in the best health. She has to avoid situations where she can get sick, she has to keep her immune system high, sleep enough, eat healthy food and avoid fast food, pops, alcohol and smoking. Unfortunately, during the preparation for treatment, under the treatment and after the embryo transfer especially, (as I mentioned before that may last for even 2 months), she shall not have even an average level of physical activity, practically nothing except walking. She shall not participate in any sports or athletic activities, such as gym workouts, swimming in an indoor/outdoor pool, riding a bike, jogging, running, tennis, aerobic, dance, etc. A woman shall be especially careful at the time of embryo retrieval and transfer and I would suggest if possible that she stays away from work as long as she can, lie in the bed, sleep a lot. All IVF clinics have an approach that for no longer than 10-20 minutes after the embryo transfer woman shall stay in bed and after she can have absolutely normal activities. I followed that advice, and after the embryo transfers I went straight to work and I didn't do anything different in my life than usual, except that I was not engaged in any physical activities, I was not carrying weight (not even from the supermarket), I was not having bathtubs and I was not using perfume or deodorant. I was eating healthy food and I was not consuming alcohol or smoking, but that was part of my usual life style. My only "bad habit" that I could not give up was coffee. However, now I think that some of these old times stories about women who maintained their pregnancies by laying in bed, not moving too much, and living in some sort of incubation, shall actually be applied for IVF after the embryo transfer, at least for the first few days which are critical for the embryo implantation, when woman is actually going through the early pregnancy.

Relieving and/or Eliminating Stress

Removing as much stress as possible from their lives is important for the couple in IVF, but it is especially important for the female patient. She has to change and sacrifice a lot of her routine and normal life. She has to spend a lot of her time and energy on the protocols—time and energy that she could have spent on other activities that she might have far preferred. More often than not, she will not be able to arrive at work on time on the days when she has a treatment, and she will have to take vacation days and sick days because of IVF. It may cost her not only promotion at work, as it happened to me, but she may even lose her job. Employers certainly prefer employees who always come on time, work consistent hours and and even extra hours, over the employees who come late to work and use flexible hours or even sick days too often. Work environment is pretty cruel in western world and female patient may suffer at work because of IVF, in many different ways such as: lack of respect and even humiliation from co-workers and boss, being passed for the more challenging assignments, not being involved in leadership, decision making process, supervising, development. Ideally female patient shall either not work or shall work part time, or from home, at least in the period when she is going through the intensive IVF schedule. Also, she cannot plan vacations or other events ahead of time, because it is unpredictable which cycle will look good to go ahead with IVF treatment. She cannot swim, exercise, or practice any sport during IVF treatments, especially after the embryo transfer. She will be too exhausted to feel up to maintaining her household duties, but because of the enormous costs associated with IVF, she probably cannot afford to have any housecleaning services or other help with her daily chores.

While struggling to have a baby, couples may feel that life is not treating them well, so they should be the ones who treat themselves well, doing things that they enjoy, that please them, and that help them avoid stress. Couples could go for leisurely walks in nature, or go to the theater or to concert, or have a romantic night out, or spend a weekend in a beautiful natural resort. For a woman, simple things may help her relieve stress, even if only temporarily: buying new pair of shoes, some cosmetics, an issue of her favorite magazine, or a book she longs to read. Some women may need to express themselves more in order to de-stress. A woman may decide to tell her partner/ husband that she needs her personal time, and she wants him to help more at home or with the child/children they may already have. Male partners' anxiety should not be underestimated, but the depression and tiredness caused by repetitive fertility treatments is borne far more by the woman: it is a burden on her body and spirit. The woman is the one who must undergo the hormone protocols, the one who is at the clinic almost every day, and the one who has to develop healthy eggs, and hopefully, healthy embryos. Her peace of mind, emotional well-being, and physical health are essential to the success of IVF and the heath of the future child.

It is better if the couple, especially the woman undergoing IVF, is not under any stress about the financial aspect of the fertility treatments. I recommend finding a way to obtain financing for IVF in some way that does not add additional stress to the process. A couple could borrow money from relatives; if that is not possible, another option is to consider "downsizing" their lifestyle. While undergoing fertility treatments, I do not recommend that the woman change jobs or try for a promotion, as long as she feels secure and relatively stress-free in her current job. A woman undergoing IVF has to make becoming a mother her top priority, and her career may have to suffer in the process. A career can be reestablished in the future, but reproductive potential cannot. It is probably ideal for any woman undergoing IVF to take a leave of absence from work so that she can concentrate only on IVF; meanwhile, her male partner can hunt for promotions, find a better-paying job, work overtime, and or get a second job.

Thinking Positively

"Why me? Why us?" These questions persist for couples struggling with infertility. However, thinking this way for a prolonged period of time will not accomplish anything; in fact, it leads us nowhere. We all have this impulse to "bewail our fate" sometimes, and it is normal and expected, especially in times of hardship, stress, and pain, but couples undergoing IVF must try to keep their thoughts and attitudes positive. At this moment on our planet, we are actually blessed to have ART. It is less than forty years since IVF was invented and about fifteen years since the ICSI method was developed. Look at how much progress we've made! If the couple experiencing infertility nowadays had lived during the time when their parents were starting a family, they probably would have had to remain biologically childless.

Education about IVF, Especially Treatment Protocols

It is important for every couple to be aware of the details of the infertility diagnosis sooner rather than later; especially in the case of male infertility, which probably takes longer time to be determined. Research statistics claim that the reasons for infertility for couples come almost 50 percent from the woman's side and 50 percent from the man's side. Unfortunately, in many societies male infertility "doesn't exist"; which is to say that it is hidden because it is considered shameful for a man. Couples experiencing infertility should be well-informed and well-educated about IVF in general, in order to be able to understand and discuss issues with their doctors; they need to be proactive, not passive, patients. They have to understand facts and odds, not leave ambiguities unexplained, and even ask for a second opinion. Patients must stay focused and well-informed, because they have to listen to professional opinions and advice. They should not hesitate to ask for clarification, to request that doctors, nurses, and clinic staff repeat instructions, and to obtain estimates of the expected outcome of the protocol, as well as precedents, the possibility of changing the protocol, etc. The highest priority of couples undergoing IVF should be to be very well-informed and to investigate their infertility problem and ART methods in general, because in the end, they will be the ones who have to make the final decisions.

Certain websites and books offer advice on how much a fertility patient should get involved in the IVF process. There are opposite opinions. One opinion advises the patient's not getting too involved, not following up with clinics to learn about the results, not asking too many questions, and not interfering with doctors' decisions. The point here is that getting too involved will only add stress and anxiety to an already very stressful process. I definitely do not agree this approach. I even deeply regret that during the first years of my fertility struggle, I didn't know the basic facts and relied entirely on the clinic staff and doctors. I was brainless, I was relaxed, and I believed that I should put my fate in their hands, because if I did, the results I wanted would come. But someone may question my previous statement, saying that thanks to being relaxed and not stressed at the very beginning of my IVF struggle, I conceived. And this is a good example of the most obvious problem with ART: every approach and statement has two sides, and both can be questioned. That makes the decision making left to the patient at the end of the process even more difficult and stressful.

The couple has to pay close attention to the instructions they are given at the clinic, and they should not expect the clinic staff to babysit them. Most often, the clinic staff understands and empathizes with the patients, but not always in the way that patients might expect, because, naturally, every couple coping with infertility feels that the problem is the biggest one in the world. We all tend to feel that way about our problems because they are ours. However, for clinic staffs, every couple is just one of many couples treated in their clinic. Also, clinic employees are still only human beings. Accountants sometimes do erroneous tax returns, doctors make wrong diagnoses, contractors cut corners in home renovations, etc. Fertility doctors and other clinic staff may also make mistakes; they are not an exception to the rule of human beings making mistakes simply because they are medical professionals. The clinic staff is just doing their work every day, and most of the time, they are very busy; if a certain day is a milestone for a couple, the staff may not even know about it. The couple should be well-organized and focused during the IVF treatment. Clinic staff may not always remind patient what to do and when to do it. Patients must double-check all the instructions, drug quantities, time for injections, and time for blood work, ultrasounds, etc., because errors may occur even in the instructions given by the clinic staff. I suggest that patients always make sure that they understood all the instructions, and if not sure, that they call the nurse, or even the doctor, in order to clarify anything ambiguous. I also recommend always checking the quantity of drugs obtained from the clinic or pharmacy, and making sure that the medication dispensed will be enough until the next visit to the clinic. However, I do not recommend ordering drugs in excess of the amount prescribed. Having drugs stocked up may lead to a financial loss as a result of expiration of the medication or a change in prescriptions.

Counseling

Extremely important advice for couples is to go through counseling sessions together from the very beginning of the fertility battle, and to do it regularly. Counselors can help couples to see the "big picture," to keep things in perspective, and to give appropriate advice and suggestions regarding the next steps, decisions, and course of action. Counseling may help couples to question their ideas, decisions, and wishes. Counselors may also notice the traps that partners get themselves into with IVF—such as a lack of Plan B, different wishes and expectations on the part of each person, etc.—and consequently, may warn couples about the potential consequences. And counselors can also be objective witnesses to couples' feelings and attitudes, so that in the future one party cannot claim that something was said, accepted, agreed to, misunderstood, and so on. I do not recommend that the female patient goes alone to counseling sessions. Women don't have to handle the entire burden of the IVF struggle on their own, all the physical and emotional tasks and responsibilities, including the importance of and need for counseling—plus the work of going through counseling.

Support from Family and Friends

Going through the IVF struggle can be difficult for couples, especially because, typically, there are not too many people that they can share the infertility problem with. Their parents might not be alive, or they might live far away or be too old to provide support; siblings and close friends might be too busy with their own lives. And most people do not have any idea what coping with infertility is really like: difficult, complicated, time-consuming, and emotionally exhausting.

For all these reasons, as well as any others specific to them, couples may also choose to keep their infertility private. If deciding to keep infertility private, as my husband and I did, I strongly recommend finding at least one person that each partner, or the couple, can openly talk to and comfortably share their experiences with. This is extremely important for stress relief, and also for hearing an objective opinion from someone who is not personally involved. (Note that this kind of advice and support is entirely different from counseling, and even if the couple shares the infertility experience with family or friends, counseling is still crucial.) When opening up in this manner, it is not necessary to disclose the whole history of the infertility struggle; the couple should share as much, or as little, as feels comfortable. Once couples open up, they may be quite surprised to discover how many other people have their own stories of experiencing infertility. The point is, couples should not feel that they have to keep it entirely as a secret.

Time, Project, and Risk Management

I suggest that couples think of IVF as a project, with the female patient as the project manager. They can think of the male partner as the project manager's assistant, or as some other type of support staff. Viewed in this way, doctors and clinic staff become consultants or technical team members; they have a lot of expertise and knowledge, but they still "report" to the project manager. Project managers typically do not know all the specific technical issues involved, but based on the information (in this case, medical) that they receive from team experts, they are able to make decisions and lead the project. The female patient, as the project manager, manages deliverables, makes decisions, and handles one of the most important aspects of the project: the time frame.

The sooner couples realize that they should consider coping with their fertility problems as a full-time job, the better. In addition to finding that they will minimize stress, they will probably increase their chance of succeeding. They need to stay focused and do the right things at the right time, and more often than not, this involves a lot of multitasking. How easy it is to waste valuable fertile time! And this is something couples need to avoid wherever possible.

Consider this scenario: A woman is thirty-five years old, and she and her male partner have just discovered that they might have a fertility problem, as they have tried to conceive naturally for the last two years. The couple calls the woman's gynecologist, but they can't get an appointment for two weeks. They go to the doctor, who gives them a referral to a fertility clinic, and again they have to wait two weeks for an appointment. At that clinic, which only performs IUI and other less-invasive protocols (not including IVF), the couple has to go through initial examinations, which take one to three months. Other delays follow. By the time the couple is ready to undergo the first fertility treatment, the woman is already thirty-six years old.

For the next year, and perhaps even longer, the couple undergoes IUI treatments and/or other protocols, not including IVF protocols. Because the woman is still in her midthirties and does not yet have an infertility diagnosis, doctors do not recommend IVF. Another year passes. The woman is now thirty-seven, and she starts to consider IVF treatments. After the first appointment with the IVF clinic, for which the wait time was a few months, the couple has to go through orientation in the new clinic, along with initial examinations and tests. The woman will have to undergo laparoscopy, which will take another three to six months, including a waiting period. When the couple undergoes their first IVF treatment, the woman is already thirty-eight. Both partners are very stressed-out and frustrated, and they regret all the time wasted. For another two years, the IVF treatments fail, and by this time, the woman is already forty. The couple decides to take a break until the next year, when the woman is forty-one. However, when she returns to the clinic, her FSH is elevated, and the doctors suggest that she proceeds with a donor-egg protocol.

At that point, the couple becomes very depressed; they may even panic. They start investigating donor-eggs procedures, as well as child adoption. They realize that there is a long waiting list, and if they are lucky, they may end up with an adopted child or a child from a donor egg, but neither one will happen for at least another two years (at which time the woman will be forty-three). They feel old and tired, exhausted both physically and mentally. The couple is concerned about whether they will be able to care for and raise a small child now that they are already in their forties, especially after the infertility battle has so depleted their physical, mental, and emotional energy.

Consider the same scenario, but move the time frame back just one or two years, and the odds of a successful outcome would be much better. After only one year of trying to conceive, the couple starts to feel concerned about possible fertility problems. The woman is thirty-four. Instead of spending two years investigating and undergoing treatments other than IVF, they try noninvasive ART (hormonal stimulation, IUI, etc.) for just one year, and then, when the woman is thirty-five, they are at the IVF clinic, ready to go through the orientation and examination. They are then able to start their first IVF treatment when the woman thirty-six, instead of thirty-eight. A difference of two years in the woman's age may be crucial to the success of any fertility treatment. The couple will also have a larger window of time in which to work. That will allow them to take short breaks, and it will allow the woman time to get her body back to its normal hormonal routine in between IVF treatments. Also, when undergoing fertility treatments while in her midthirties, the woman will be far more relaxed and optimistic, instead of feeling stressed-out, nervous, and even panicked, as she will when age forty or older.

Risk management (the calculation of risks versus problems) can easily assist couples going through IVF, just as it can be helpful when applied to any other circumstances in life. Risk is hypothetical, but it can be predicted, defined, and evaluated as low, medium, or high. By appropriately addressing the risk, any can significantly lower the risk probability and thereby improve the chance of achieving the desired outcome. On the other hand, when risk (predicted or not) materializes, it becomes a problem. And dealing with the problem is much more difficult than anticipating and dealing with risk (if predictable). Plus, once a problem arises and requires resolution, there is far less likelihood of succeeding with the original goal.

Therefore, the earlier the couple starts applying the principles of time, project, and risk management in their fertility battle, the sooner they may get some positive results, whether that means having their own biological/genetic baby or babies, deciding to have donor-egg or surrogate babies, choosing to adopt, or deciding to remain childless. However, the biggest challenge is being able to apply these logical, rational principles into a process that is so deeply emotional.

How to Choose an IVF Clinic

I recommend that at some point during the fertility struggle, neither at the very beginning nor after too much time has passed, the couple ask their family doctor (or the woman's gynecologist) for a referral to a few fertility clinics in the area (if they are lucky to have more than one clinic nearby). Couples will spend a lot of extra time going to appointments at different clinics (and maybe even doing cycle monitoring in some), but the time spent is valuable because they will get a sense of each clinic and have a chance to talk to several doctors and clinic staff members. The benefit will be in getting better educated about ART, in hearing different doctors' opinions, and also from having the opportunity to evaluate different doctors' answers to the same questions (that is, seeing whether they receive the same or different answers). All these conversations may bring the couple closer to the decision about which type of protocol to choose, and about their next steps, whether toward more fertility treatments, termination of IVF, and/or choosing other options for having children.

Apart from each couple's own gut feelings, there are some factors that may help them choose a fertility clinic. The recommendations that follow include the most important ones, based on my experience.

Get a Recommendation from Another Patient

This is probably one of the best ways to learn more about a clinic. But keep in mind that there is not much objectivity if the recommendation comes from a couple who conceived in that clinic. It will sound like the doctors in that clinic are the most knowledgeable and that the clinic is the best clinic in the world.

Meet the Doctors

The couple's impression of the fertility doctors and their advice and recommendations will have a great influence on the decision of which clinic to choose. Here are some key questions to ask: How many years of experience with ART does each doctor have? What protocol(s) do the doctors suggest, based on the history of the couple (or female patient)? Do the doctors clearly explain the medical/scientific facts and the couple's realistic expectations for success? Do the doctors suggest some new protocol, or do they recommend a modification to the existing protocol? Do they explain the reasons for this recommendation? Do the doctors describe the results of research done at that clinic, as well as sharing new scientific discoveries and statistics from other medical/scientific organizations? Do the doctors love and feel passionate about their work, and do they empathy toward the couple (female patient)?

Examine the Clinic

Look at the clinic premises. Is it well-organized, clean, and patient-friendly? Do the staff members seem disciplined about their work? Are they focused and attentive, or do they appear disorganized, nervous, lacking knowledge? Do staff members give contradictory information and/or forget to provide important information? Is the clinic staff professional, kind, and empathetic?

Location of the Clinic

Another important factor in choosing a clinic is its location. I suggest choosing a clinic that is close to the woman's workplace, if she works, or halfway between home and work, as there will be many days when she will arrive at work late. The minimum time spent at the clinic during a protocol and while undergoing cycle monitoring is two hours per day. Typically, every two to five days during IVF treatment, the woman needs to come to the clinic, but sometimes she may need to go on consecutive days, even as many as ten days per protocol, not including the days of egg retrieval and embryo transfer. For the female patient, that is easily fifteen to twenty hours per treatment spent in the clinic, not including travel time, and not including the additional five to ten hours for egg retrieval and transfer.

Waiting Time at the Clinic

Another important parameter to consider is the waiting time for a first appointment at the clinic, as well as the regular daily waiting time. If the couple gets an initial appointment with the clinic within a short time frame, it is a good sign; however, if the clinic cannot schedule the first appointment until three months (or more) from when the couple calls, that is a serious indication that the clinic already has too many patients or that it is not efficiently run. Clinics that are understaffed or too busy cannot provide optimal patient care; daily waiting time at such clinics will likely be longer as well.

Different Types of Fertility Doctors

There are several types of fertility doctors, and I have listed them below, in alphabetical order. To make it simple, let's consider these doctor types as male, other than the "female doctor" designation. This categorization is my personal judgment only, on my personal beliefs, emotions, intuition, and experience interacting with numerous fertility specialists. Please also realize that I have deliberately included a bit of humor and sarcasm in the descriptions of the different types of fertility doctors.

The Businessman

This one was the first in town to open an IVF clinic. He is always first in implementing new methods, new protocols, new discoveries, and new medications. He regularly attends professional meetings and conferences, and he is always busy writing his own reports. He may also fall into the "statistics hunter" category.

Pros

If a couple has already tried all the standard and conservative methods, this doctor might be a good fit. Anyone who wants to discuss brand-new and different approaches will find this doctor appealing. If looking for a doctor who believes in success, this one will be the best option.

Cons

This doctor is not often present in the clinic, and he does not play an active role in treatments and procedures. He tends to focus more on the higher level of managing the clinic, researching new IVF discoveries and approaches, and going to conferences, and leaves other doctors and/or clinic staff to deal with the patients. Patients have to be careful with the decisions and recommendations given both by the "businessman" doctor and his assistants, as there is a great likelihood of poor communications and/or miscommunications. The "businessman" may give his advice without having enough input as to patients' actual responses to IVF protocols. His assistants and staff may not have enough information on patients' overall infertility history, and so they may not be able to look at the "big picture"; in addition, the staff may not feel knowledgeable about new methods and/or approaches, which will prevent them from feeling comfortable discussing and implementing them.

The Charlatan

This doctor does not go explain the science of fertility treatments with any depth. There is more of a sense that he found a good, secure, and growing field for his medical practice.

Pros

If the couple has a minor fertility problem and the female patient is young, it's worth trying some of the noninvasive infertility methods that this doctor might recommend and/or implement.

Cons

If the infertility problem persists, even after many attempts with IUI or other noninvasive methods, this doctor has nothing more to offer other than a referral to a fertility clinic specializing in IVF. If the recommendation to cancel IUI (or other noninvasive infertility protocol) does not come from this doctor in a reasonable period of time, depending on the patient's condition and age, she will have to be very careful, as a prolonged amount of time spent with this doctor may result in a decline in her fertility, with time, health, energy, and money wasted.

The Doctor-in-Training

This doctor is right out of school, with little to no practical experience; often he will be from another region, state, or even another country.

Pros

He is definitely interested in the field, and he adds value to the clinic. He may bring some experience from the places where he received his education and training (medical internship, residency, etc.). Usually, he is young and eager, and can devote a lot of time to the clinic. He is ambitious and keen on studying patient files in detail.

Cons

He may be nervous and scared when it comes to the decision-making process. He is also not very experienced in legal matters, so he doesn't want to risk making decisions that might not be "by the book," which results in his more conservative approach. He would rather leave any difficult decisions to the senior doctor or the clinic director.

The Female Doctor

As stated previously, most fertility doctors are male. The basic pros and cons of female doctors fit the same basic description.

Pros

If the female patient feels uncomfortable being examined and treated for infertility by a male doctor, a woman fertility doctor could be the best option. The female patient may get lucky and have a female doctor that is nice, kind, and empathetic, as well as knowledgeable and skilled.

Cons

Women fertility doctors may not necessarily be more sympathetic to the female patient's situation than their male counterparts, even though most female patients will likely expect and wish that this will be the case. It simply depends upon each individual doctor. The doctor might be a woman who had her children when she was much younger than the patient, and she might "blame" the patient for delaying her own motherhood and being ignorant as to her fertility potential. Or the doctor may have issues about her own infertility and/or be childless for other reasons, neither of which will necessarily make her compassionate. Conversely, any of these scenarios might make her extremely compassionate and empathetic.

The Male Chauvinist

The description of this category is self-evident.

Pros

Regardless of the doctors' direct or indirect attitude to women, they are helping females to have children.

Cons

In my opinion, unfortunately, most fertility doctors, although dealing primarily with women, are, in fact, male chauvinists. Why do I think so? Because no doctor told me while I was in my mid and late thirties that I might easily end up not having kids, despite the fact that I was never diagnosed with infertility and was in IVF primarily because of my husband's infertility. During the time when I still had some fertility potential, no doctor ever told me to try some less-aggressive methods (IUI, for example) with donor sperm; however, when my fertility drastically declined, they did tell me to switch to donor eggs! Most of them suggested having a donor-egg baby, as if that would be an easy and natural decision, as if it were just a matter of surfing the Internet to find a donor and having enough money to finance the procedure.

In one of my husband's and my nasty conversations, when we were already deep into our marital/family crisis and my husband was trying to force me to conceive with donor eggs, he said in cynical tone, "The fertility doctors are suggesting donor eggs without any hesitation and concerns that they might hurt a woman's feelings because, obviously, here in North America, it is very normal and common."

Only once did a doctor mention to me, in humorous tone, that one of my options would be to hook up with the "milkman"; that was during the last phase of my journey through IVF, when I was already approaching age forty-three. As my fertility had already seriously declined by that point, even if I had managed to do it with the "milkman," the likelihood of success would have been zero—it was already too late.

The Obstetrician/Gynecologist (OB/GYN)

This doctor has been in the field from the day he started his practice. It's his work, and it's his life. He also sees hundreds of pregnant women, and he continually monitors their pregnancies and delivers their babies. He will be straightforward with the patient, providing scientific—and experience-based facts.

Pros

This doctor is very experienced and knowledgeable. He may not necessarily know or agree with new and "hot" stuff in fertility treatments, as he wants to see how well it will work over time. He has to feel comfortable with a new protocol before deciding to implement it in his fertility clinic. On the other hand, his wide knowledge and experience with so many different cases, through his long years of practice, are of a great value and give him confidence in using his expertise to treat infertility and to make the best decisions for every patient.

Cons

The fact that this doctor holds hundreds of newborns every year may not help the patient, as he may never hold the patient's baby. If the patient experiences numerous unsuccessful treatments led by this doctor, who is probably following a predominantly conservative approach, it might be time for the patient to change doctors. A patient does not have time to wait until this doctor feels comfortable implementing some new IVF approaches and methods.

Prince Charming

This doctor might also be thought of as the "woman's favorite"; he is nice, kind, and warm. He treats each patient as if she were the only patient in the clinic. He has enough time to chat with the patient, to explain every single detail, to answer all the patient's questions, and to comment on the patient's ideas. He is cheerful when examining the patient during the ultrasounds, looking, counting, and commenting on the patient's follicles. He sings a "good luck song" when transferring embryos.

Pros

Patient will not feel stressed-out when coming to this clinic. In fact, the patient's optimism will rise, and she can actually "see" the photo of this doctor holding her newborn posted on the board in the waiting room of the clinic.

Cons

When things go wrong and the patient's IVF treatment fails, the patient's disappointment might be even deeper than it otherwise would be. This doctor may not appear as warm and nice as before, as he might discern that the patient feels misled by his easygoing and optimistic approach.

The Scientist

This doctor is fertility/reproduction scientist. He likes to challenge nature, and the pinnacle of his professional and personal satisfaction comes when he succeeds in doing that.

Pros

Science is powerful, and the patient has to rely on it, especially if the fertility problem is serious and cannot be cured with any methods other than aggressive IVF/ICSI treatments. With this doctor, the patient will be offered the opportunity to go beyond any prior options (testing genetic content in eggs and sperm, testing embryos in the lab, etc.) All this research and investigation may help provide patient and doctor with more information, and maybe even a clue about the reason for repeated unsuccessful fertility treatments.

Cons

By allowing this doctor to experiment with them, the couple might be getting themselves into a high-risk situation, without a guarantee that they will ever have their baby. After the cycle monitoring and investigation phase, which may take a couple of months, this doctor may come to the conclusion that the patient is not responding the way he had hoped and that he cannot implement his new scientific approach on the patient. Also, he may treat one of the patient's problems successfully but mess up something else. The patient may end up with the sense that it was a "successful surgery, but the patient died." Plus, if the experimental treatment fails, the patient may end up feeling like one of the doctor's guinea pigs, but with nothing positive to show for it.

The Serious Doctor

This doctor takes his engagement in fertility treatments way too seriously. He never smiles, and he does not offer the patient too much hope. He looks more like he works in funeral home rather than a fertility clinic where babies could be conceived. Usually, he is too straightforward, leaving no hope that a miracle could happen.

Pros

Patient may feel extra confident when seeing that this doctor is not in a "take it easy" mode. Patient may also feel especially confident that this doctor will do his best, will not allow any mistakes to happen, and will not leave any gray areas or ambiguities up to chance.

Cons

This doctor may pass his seriousness and pessimism on to the couple, who probably already have more than they ever wanted. Their problems may then appear even worse to them after their conversations with this doctor. But it may also help the couple to be more realistic, and if they are in the early stage and filled with too much optimism, that dose of seriousness may be helpful. If they are in the later stages, the doctor's pessimism may help them to consider stopping fertility treatments, considering alternative options, and/or moving on.

Statistics Hunter

This doctor is interested in the best business results and, perhaps, even some fame in the IVF world. His goal is for his clinic to achieve amazing statistics. He may also fall into the "businessman" category.

Pros

It's possible that, driven by a desire for the best statistics, this doctor will implement all the best methods, have the best-trained staff, invest in the best facilities, and so on, and then the couple might benefit and become a part of his "good numbers"!

Cons

It is possible that, after getting acquainted with the couple's history, this doctor may brutally reject them for treatment in his clinic; if he estimates that their likelihood of succeeding with IVF is very low, which could ruin his overall success rates, he will probably reject them in such a fashion. The only condition under which "problem" patients may be offered the opportunity to receive treatment in such a clinic would be if they are willing to use donor eggs or donor sperm, consider having a surrogate baby, or availing themselves of other options, depending on her specific case.

How We Managed Our Finances during the IVF Years: Tips on Saving Money for Fertility Treatments

Fertility treatments are enormously expensive, and this becomes especially problematic if both partners are not working full-time and have no financial help from family or friends. It is extremely difficult unless at least one partner has medical insurance coverage through his or her employer, as this will usually cover some percentage of the cost of the fertility drugs. The cost of the fertility drugs may amount to more than 50 percent of the total cost of treatment. If couple does not have a medical plan that covers fertility drugs, and many plans don't, the expenses incurred on the drugs, combined with the rest of the couple's medical expenses, may be claimed on the couple's tax return (depends on the regulations in the country where couple lives).

Couples may want to investigate the best options for loans to use solely for medical expenses and to pay out over an extended period of time. Many clinics provide referrals to financial institutions offering such loans. In some countries government may provide help for financing ART, or even have ART procedures covered by regular medical insurance coverage. Couples may also wish to consider paying the minimum mortgage payment and using the equity credit line. They may consider downsizing their living space, which is a difficult decision. However, once they decide to stop fertility treatments—whether because they have a child through IVF or adoption, or because they just decide that the time for IVF closure has come—they will be able to catch up with their finances, gradually returning money to the banks, relatives, friends, and so on.

[AUTHOR'S NOTE: *As with the medical and scientific information described throughout this book, information on insurance, tax filing, finances, etc., are purely based on my own experience and opinion. Seek appropriate professional advice for understanding the details of insurance coverage, tax filing, finances, etc.*]

I will recommend some ways and tips for how to save money in order to cover the cost of IVF, at least to some extent. Sticking to a budget and saving as much as possible will certainly be easier for couples who are very motivated to have kids through IVF, and who do not resent all the sacrifices they will have to make, including downsizing their lifestyle, reducing their comfort level, and their lowering financial and social status.

It is very difficult to make the decision to stop treating yourself to things you enjoy (especially for women undergoing IVF protocols). In addition to all that women go through during the treatments, they must now endure the additional stress of saving money for IVF. One of my preferred stress reliefs while going through IVF was shopping. It was an extra challenge to watch to curb my spending and limit my shopping budget while simultaneously enjoying the short-term stress relief from IVF that I found in shopping malls. When shopping for clothes and shoes, for example, I learned how to look for items that would last more than only one season, that were of a good quality and classic style, and I waited until the end of the season so that I could buy them at half price. (I soon discovered that that the best shopping deals and sales were usually in January, February, and August.)

Sometimes I felt sad and frustrated when thinking that I would not have my dream house, or even a renovated kitchen and bathroom, by the time I turned fifty. Or even worse, that I would end up living in a small and old house forever. I couldn't even think about home renovation, addition to the house, or moving to a bigger, newer, and nicer house. I could not even afford to buy new furniture or redecorate. But I did find a way to enhance our home interior in small, inexpensive ways. I developed a technique of passionate shopping for inexpensive, sometimes vintage, and attractive, unique home décor items. To create a fresh new look, I would buy inexpensive new sheers, lamps, clocks, mirrors, paintings, and so on. Once in a while, I would even find some nice pieces of furniture in vintage shops, and once I refurbished them, they looked wonderful. I bought cracked sculptures, broken vases, lamps with missing pieces, and all sorts of such things, and then I fixed them. I also bought some beautiful picture frames, and then I framed our family photos, as well as our daughter's artwork and diplomas. I painted the interior walls of the house myself, and the new color gave our home a whole new look. That motivated me to spruce up the outside. I couldn't renovate our yard with fancy stone statues, waterfalls, and fountains, but I could still make it beautiful by planting new flowers and starting my own vegetable garden. I share all this not to go overboard with details about my household projects, but to show that there are ways to fix and change things without spending a lot of money. An additional benefit is that the activities may distract the couple/woman from the constant focus on IVF, as well as all the stress that entails.

And then there was holiday shopping on a budget. I would usually start shopping for Christmas gifts in October and finish in November. I became a master of "regifting" the candle holders, jewelry boxes, and similar gifts that we received from other people, but that we either didn't like or didn't need. Sometimes I found that I didn't like or never wore a new piece of clothing or a pair of shoes, and so I would give these never-worn items away as Christmas gifts or birthday presents.

I saved on electronic devices, such as cell phones and PDAs, by being the last person in North America who did not have a cell phone (it certainly felt that way). When our daughter reached the age when she wanted to watch TV, I soon realized how addictive it was for children. I canceled our cable subscription, letting her watch some movies and TV series on DVD (and later on the Internet and Netflix). Although the original intention for this was not saving money but ensuring that she had quality time and spend enough time outdoors playing, we saved a considerable amount of money by not subscribing to cable TV.

In truth, the only one that I didn't want to save money on was our daughter. I wanted her to have the nicest crib, nicest bed cover, nicest pillow, nicest baby stroller, nicest high chair, nicest light in the room, nicest pacifiers with music, nicest girls' clothes, nicest girls' shoes, nicest backpacks, nicest bike, nicest skates, nicest skis, nicest everything. I never bought anything for her from the vintage store. I wanted her to have lots of toys, books, and Christmas gifts. However, when buying toys for her, I realized that sometimes the most expensive toys were the least creative and not as interesting for the child as some of the cheaper toys could be. One set of Lego or one cheap clay set can keep a kid engaged for a couple of hours, while a fancy expensive doll may stay under the pile of toys and be forgotten for years. When our daughter reached the age of four, she preferred interactive games, and it was more important to her to have company to play with than to have toys. I didn't buy her too many books, but I often took her to the library, where we frequently borrowed as many books as she chose.

The following table shows some examples, ideas and tips of how to save money by regularly sticking to a budget and reducing spending by eliminating/curtailing some unnecessary items, such as services, shopping, entertainment, vacations, and so on. It is based on the approximate cost of living in North America in period 2010-2013 for a couple without kids, with both partners working, having a monthly net income of $6,000 (without extra source of income). Assumption is that there are two IVF treatments per year, cost is $6,000 for each and there is an additional cost of $5,000 for drugs, which makes an annual expense for fertility treatments of $17,000. Assumption is that at least one partner has health insurance/benefits plan at work which includes life insurance, dental plan, medical plan, drug plan, but not including fertility drugs coverage.

In the following table it is not included: tax return based on deduction of medical expenses and government financial help for infertility treatments that may exist in certain countries.

In the left part of the table (page 106) is shown that a North American couple with an annual net income of $72,000 and the over-spending life style is ending up with $10,000 debt annually, even without extra expenses for IVF. With the additional cost for IVF same couple gets into the annual debt of $27,000.

In the right part of the table (page 107), it is shown how the same couple may apply some restrictions to the spending and some downsizing to the life style. That may bring them into the minimum or no debt, even with the expenses for IVF. If the annual debt still occurs it can be carried over through some bank loans, credit lines, or credit cards. There are also some financial agencies which are providing loans for infertility treatments.

HOW TO KEEP CONTROL OVER THE BUDGET AND HOW TO SAVE MONEY FOR FERTILITY TREATMENTS
(for the North American couple without kids, both partners are employed)

© Anastasia Sputnik, 2013

DESCRIPTION OF THE EXPENSE (based on period 2010-2013 in North America)	EXPENSE (in US or Canadian dollar)	ANNUAL SPENDING (without the budget watch)
Food	$850 spent per month	$10,200.00
Personal hygene and cosmetics	$100 spent per month	$1,200.00
Dinning out 2 times per month	2 times $60 per month	$1,440.00
Business lunch	2 times per month $30 per lunch (each partner)	$1,440.00
Fast food, coffee	2 times per week $12 (each partner)	$2,400.00
Movie theatres, concerts, theatres, other entertainment	3 times per month $80	$2,880.00
TV cable	$30 monthly	$360.00
Cell phone plans	$60 monthly for each partner	$1,440.00
Internet; home phone with voice mail and call waiting	$80 per month	$960.00
Allowance for the new technology, Iphone, Ipad, tablet, lap top, computer	$700 annually	$700.00
Extra cost for bank statements, banking service fees etc.	$20 per month	$240.00
Interests paid on credit cards and loans	total debt of $10,000 with 18% interest rates on credit card	$1,800.00
Mortgage or rent	based on $1,500 for 400K mortgage	$18,000.00
Property tax, utility bills, condo fees	$4,500 property tax annually; $300 per month for home bills	$8,100.00
Home and car insurance	$150 monthly	$1,800.00
Different home services (computer maintenance, plumber, electrician, roof repair, gardener, etc.)	allowance $100 per month	$1,200.00
Home cleaning	$250 per month	$3,000.00
Dry cleaning	$80 per month	$960.00
Parking	$150 monthly for each partner	$3,600.00
Gas	$300 monthly	$3,600.00
Monthly allowance for new clothes/shoes	$200 monthly (total for both partners)	$2,400.00
Monthly allowance for home cleaning supplies, house improvements and appliances	$200 monthly	$2,400.00
Gym fees, sport club fees, other memberships	$130 monthly	$1,560.00
Magazine subscriptions and books	$40 for subscriptions and $180 for buying books annually	$220.00
Hairdresser, manicure, pedicure, waxing, massage, spa	$200 for both partners spent in 2 months	$1,200.00
Vacation (1st week)	1 week all inclusive vacation in high season (for two)	$1,800.00
Vacation (2nd week)	1 week travelling overseas or to the other town/province (for two)	$4,000.00
Mini vacations and long weekends in natural resorts, visiting other towns, skiing weekends, festivals etc.	$300 allowance in two months for two	$1,800.00
Christmas gifts		$500.00
Health, drugs, dental, optical, orthotic, life insurance (at least one partner has medical plan at work)	additional life and/or critical illness insurance for woman undergoing IVF	$700.00
Donations		$100.00
Additional spending		
Additional spending		
TOTAL SPENDING ANNUALLY (without closely watching budget/expenditures, resulting in carry over debt of $10,000 on credit cards, annually)		$82,000.00
COST OF FERTILITY TREATMENTS (based on 2 IVFs per year, each $6,000 and $5,000 per year for drugs)		$17,000.00
TOTAL SPENDING ANNUALLY WITH THE MEDICAL EXPENSES INCLUDED (without closely watching budget/expenditures)		$99,000.00
TOTAL ANNUAL NET INCOME (based on $6,000 net monthly income for couple, after tax deduction)		$72,000.00
BALANCE (DEBT)		-$27,000.00

DESCRIPTION OF SAVINGS/DOWNSIZING	ANNUAL SPENDING (with the budget watch)	SAVINGS (annually)
Shop in the cheaper supermarket and look for the sale items and coupons, try $800 per month	$9,600.00	$600.00
Shop in the cheaper store and look for the sale items and coupons, try $80 per month	$960.00	$240.00
Dine out just on special occasions (once in 2 months)	$360.00	$1,080.00
Reduce the frequency of business lunch	$480.00	$960.00
Prepare lunch at home for 5 out of 7 week days; become a member of the coffee club at work; allowance of $15 weekly (each partner)	$1,500.00	$900.00
Go out once per month; consider going just for a walk, or renting movie at home, or inviting guests for dinner	$960.00	$1,920.00
Cancel TV and switch to Netflix or similar, $10 monthly	$120.00	$240.00
Downsize cell phone services to $50 per month per person	$1,200.00	$240.00
Cancel voice mail and call waiting and get the old fashion type of phone	$400.00	$560.00
Buy an older version of the product or wait until the fancy new technology goes on sale	$500.00	$200.00
Cancel all unnecessary fees and switch to the Internet banking	$120.00	$120.00
Switch to the credit card or credit line with the interest rate of 5%	$500.00	$1,300.00
Shop for the better interest rates on mortgage, or if you are renting, find the cheaper apartment	$14,400.00	$3,600.00
Install energy saving lights, low pressure douche; keep heating and air conditioner low when you are not at home; savings $50 monthly	$7,500.00	$600.00
Shop for the better offer	$1,200.00	$600.00
Try to do most of it without contracting out	$500.00	$700.00
Find the cheaper provider and/or reduce from weekly to by-weekly home cleaning	$1,500.00	$1,500.00
Switch to the wrinkle free clothes, allowance $30 per month	$360.00	$600.00
At least one partner to turn to the public transport, to carpool, to bike to work, or to find a cheaper parking	$2,400.00	$1,200.00
Use public transport more; reduce to $200 per month	$2,400.00	$1,200.00
Reduce allowance to $100 monthly	$1,200.00	$1,200.00
Reduce allowance to $150 monthly	$1,800.00	$600.00
Find a cheaper membership, or consider free recreation, such as biking, jogging, swimming in the public pools etc.	$940.00	$620.00
Become a member of public library	$100.00	$120.00
Find a less expensive hairdresser or color your hair at home; cancel manicure, etc.	$600.00	$600.00
Go on one week vacation in the low season	$1,300.00	$500.00
Cancel	$0.00	$4,000.00
Stay in the motel, cheap hotel, or studio with the possibility to prepare food on your own. Go camping. Reduce days of mini vacations.	$1,100.00	$700.00
Shop for Christmas in September and October, savings can be significant	$300.00	$200.00
No savings	$700.00	$0.00
Cancel	$0.00	$100.00
Additional savings if couple has a medical plan which covers fertility drugs (through the employers' insurance and benefits plan)		
Additional savings if couple can claim a tax return after the income deduction of medical expenses		
TOTAL SPENDING ANNUALLY (with watching budget/expenditures)	**$55,000.00**	**$27,000.00**
COST OF FERTILITY TREATMENTS	**$17,000.00**	
TOTAL SPENDING ANNUALLY WITH THE MEDICAL EXPENSES INCLUDED (with watching budget/expenditures)	**$72,000.00**	
TOTAL ANNUAL NET INCOME (tax deducted)	**$72,000.00**	
BALANCE	**$0.00**	

Quiz: Are You Ready to Stop Fertility Treatments?

- Do you find yourself asking silly questions, such as:
  Does it matter, for my blood results, which arm the blood was drawn from? Does it matter if I injected the hormones fifteen minutes later than prescribed?
- Do you turn your head away when you see a pregnant woman?
- Do you turn your head away from babies and kids in strollers?
- Do you avoid seeing newborn babies?
- Do you envy any woman who is pregnant or who has child(ren)?
- When you see a pregnant woman, do you feel indifferent rather than jealous?
- Do you no longer feel bitter toward and/or envious of people pushing baby strollers, mothers nursing babies, and/or parents holding their kids' hands?
- When you imagine your newborn, do you no longer feel overwhelming joy, but instead, indifference or irritation?
- Are you starting to feel that you are too old to have a baby? Even if the baby is finally born, are you starting to fear that you might not have enough energy to care for the baby?
- Are you starting to think that you are too old to raise kids? Do you also have concerns that your kid(s) may end up living without parents at a young age and/or caring for old and possibly sick parents while still teenagers or young adults themselves?
- Do you feel convinced that even if you finally have your baby, people will think that you are not mother but grandmother to the child?
- Do you fear that even if you conceive and give birth to a child, that child might not be healthy because of your older age? Does that fear override your enthusiasm to try to conceive?
- Are you starting to be paranoid about your health? Are you surfing the Internet to read studies about the higher cancer risks for women who have undergone multiple assisted reproduction protocols? Are you constantly checking for breast lumps, or you are scared whenever you feel pain in your ovaries? Or even worse, are you convinced that you already may have some silent deadly disease?
- When you look in the mirror, does your face look sad and older, and your body big and fat because of all the weight you gained as a result of the fertility treatments? As a woman, do you feel old and unattractive?
- Do you feel that by not being able to become a mother, you are less female than other women and less valuable as a human being?
- Are you often imagining an unknown cute child, abandoned or with parents who died, who is living in poor and unhealthy conditions, and whose life, with your love and care, could change from hell to paradise?

- Do you feel abandoned by your husband, family, and friends? Do you feel that there are not too many people left in the world who understand your despair and sadness, your urge to continue the fertility struggle, and your inability to stop or find another way out?
- Do you feel that you want your life back?

If you recognize yourself in at least half of the above statements, it is maybe time to stop fertility treatments.

APPENDIX

As previously described, this Appendix includes tables outlining the details of each of the IVF protocol that I went through. I've also included a list of the medications that I was taking during IVF.

Next is a table with the Terms and Definitions, followed by the Resources (list of the Internet web sites). List of the books related to infertility that I recommend for reading follows. Finally, I am providing a template table for monitoring IVF protocols, which may help female patients to record and track their IVF treatments/protocols.

Table 1: Details about the IVF protocols during the stage "The Hopeful Beginning"

	NO. OF IVF/ICSI PROTOCOLS (INCLUDING CANCELED)	MY AGE	DATE	TYPE OF IVF/ICSI PROTOCOL	OUTCOME
		36	Winter 2001		First time seeing fertility doctor
		36	Spring 2002	**Laparoscopy**	Laparoscopy did not reveal any indication of my infertility. At the same time, my husband's sperm count of two million and low motility was confirmed.
CLINIC A	1st (canceled)	36	Summer 2002	**Long Lupron Protocol:** Lupron 0.05 and Gonal-F 250 units	Protocol canceled because of high estradiol level. Because of ovarian cysts, Minovral contraceptive pills were prescribed. Period didn't start for more than thirty days, for the first time in my menstrual history. I was given Provera, and after five days I had a period.
	2nd	37	Fall 2002	**Long Lupron Protocol:** Lupron 0.05 and Gonal-F, 225 units; from day 8 to day 13, Gonal-F increased to 300 units; progesterone suppositories after the embryo transfer	On day sixteen, retrieved four eggs; on day nineteen, transferred two embryos, with eight and five cells, A and B quality; healthy pregnancy and healthy baby born.
	3rd	39	Winter 2004-5	**Long Lupron Protocol:** Lupron 0.05 and Gonal-F 375 units; progesterone suppositories after the embryo transfer until the pregnancy test	On day fourteen, retrieved four eggs; on day seventeen, transferred two embryos, seven and four cells, B and B quality.
	4th	39	Spring 2005	**Agonist/Antagonist Protocol:** Serofen, Gonal-F 450 units per day, and Orgalutran; progesterone suppositories after the embryo transfer until the pregnancy test	On day thirteen, retrieved one egg; on day sixteen, transferred one embryo.
	5th	40	Winter 2005-6	**Long Lupron protocol**: Lupron 0.05 and Gonal-F 500 units; progesterone suppositories after the embryo transfer until the pregnancy test	On day sixteen, retrieved three eggs; on day eighteen, transferred two embryos, nine and eight cells, B and B quality.

Table 2: Details about the IVF protocols during the stage "Reality Checks on IVF"

	NO. OF IVF/ICSI PROTOCOLS (INCLUDING CANCELED)	MY AGE	DATE	TYPE OF IVF/ICSI PROTOCOL	OUTCOME
DOCTOR FOR IUI		40	Spring 2006	**Varicocele Surgery:** (husband)	No improvement on sperm number, quality, motility.
	Total of 3	40.5	Summer 2006	**IUI Protocols (3):** with no stimulation or with very low stimulation	No success.
CLINIC B	6th	41	Winter 2006-7	**Micro Flare Protocol:** Suprefact 0.05, Letrozole (Femara), Puregon 2x150 units; progesterone suppositories after the embryo transfer until the pregnancy test	On day twenty-one, retrieved three eggs; on day twenty-three, transferred two embryos, five and four cells, grade-1 quality.
	7th (canceled)	41	Spring 2007	**Micro Flare Protocol:** Suprefact 0.05, Letrozole (Femara), Repronex 2x150 units; starting to take DHEA	Canceled; one follicle was leading, and it appeared that I had already ovulated despite the ovulation suppression.
	8th	42	Winter 2007-8	**Agonist antagonist protocol:** taking DHEA 5 months before the IVF treatment; Menopur 400 units, Orgalutran; progesterone suppositories after the embryo transfer until pregnancy test; Doxycycline after the embryo transfer	The best protocol outcome in years. On day eleven retrieved two eggs; on day thirteen, transferred two embryos, eight and six cells, grade-1 quality (ultrasound scan of these embryos is shown in the chapter Introduction of Agonist/Antagonist Protocol in Clinic B; Last Good Protocol)
CLINIC C			Fall 2007		Cycle monitoring; clinic accepted us for IVF/ICSI protocol, but we decided not to go ahead.
CLINIC D		42.5	Spring 2008	**Menopause Induction with Depo Lupron:** preparation for future IVF protocol and possible improvement of uterine lining	
	9th (canceled)	42.5	Summer 2008	**Micro Flare Protocol:** Suprefact 0.05, Puregon 375, Repronex 75 units; taking DHEA	Canceled because estradiol level began dropping at the beginning of protocol.
	10th	43	Fall 2008	**Micro Flare Protocol:** Suprefact 0.05, Puregon 400, Repronex 150 units; progesterone suppositories after the embryo transfer until the pregnancy test	On day twenty-two, retrieved three eggs; on day twenty-five, no embryos transferred.

Table 3: Details about the IVF protocols during the stage "Pushing the Limits of IVF"

	NO. OF IVF/ICSI PROTOCOLS (INCLUDING CANCELED)	MY AGE		TYPE OF IVF/ICSI PROTOCOL	OUTCOME
CLINIC E	Total of 5	43	Winter 2008 and Spring 2009	**Natural Low-Stimulation Agonist/Antagonist Protocols (5):** Orgalutran or Cetrotide; Menopur or Puregon, 100 units; progesterone suppositories after the embryo transfer until the pregnancy test	During one of these protocols, four eggs retrieved and two embryos transferred.

List of Medications Used in My IVF/ICSI Protocols and during the Preparation for Protocols

BRAND NAME	TYPE OF MEDICATION
Cetrotide	gonadotropin-releasing hormone antagonists
DHEA	dehydroepiandrosterone
Depo Lupron	leuprolide
Doxycycline	antibiotic
Endometrin	vaginal suppositories (progesterone)
Folic Acid	vitamin
Gonal-F	gonadotropin
hCG injection	human chorionic gonadotropin
Femara	letrozole
Lupron	leuprolide
Marvelon	birth control pill
Materna	multivitamins
Menopur	gonadotropin
Min-Ovral	birth control pill
Orgalutran	gonadotropin-releasing hormone antagonists
Ovral	birth control pill
Prometrium	vaginal suppositories (progesterone)
Provera	progesterone
Puregon	gonadotropin
Repronex	gonadotropin
Serophene	clomiphene citrate, ovulatory agent
Suprefact	buserelin acetat

Syringes left over from my 7 years of IVF

Terms and Definitions

Listed below and collected from various Internet resources, are the definitions and explanations for most of the medical/infertility/IVF terms mentioned in this book.

[AUTHOR'S NOTE: *I do not take any responsibility for interpretation and/or understanding of the terms. I provide in these definitions some terminology and jargon used in IVF clinics by IVF professionals at the time when I attended those clinics and underwent IVF protocols. I am not the author of these definitions and am not infringing on the copyrights of the authors of the content cited from websites and other resources used. Resources that were used for the definitions of terms are listed in the section of the appendix that follows these terms and definitions.*]

Agonist protocol	GnRH agonist is a medication that works against GnRH (gonadotropin releasing hormone) in the brain. GnRH works on the pituitary gland, helping it to release follicle stimulating hormone (FSH) and luteinizing hormone (LH). These hormones play a key role in ovulation. GnRH agonists work to block the action of GnRH, preventing the release of LH and FSH, thus preventing ovulation. GnRH agonists are used to help stop ovulation from occurring too early. When ovulation occurs early, eggs tend to be of a lower quality and less useful. Agonists mentioned in this book are Lupron and Suprefact.
Antagonist protocol	Ovarian Stimulation Using GnRH-antagonists, such as Ganirelix and Cetrotide. Both kinds of drugs, antagonists and agonists, prevent LH surges (in different ways). A new approach to the poor responder involves the use of GnRH antagonists (Ganirelix Acetate Injection, Cetrotide). With this protocol, gonadotropin or FSH is started on the second or third day of the menstrual cycle, with no birth control or agonist pretreatment. High doses of FSH are utilized to maximize egg numbers. When the lead follicle reaches an average of 13 to 14 mm. in diameter, an antagonist is administered to avoid a premature LH surge while gonadotropins are continued. Some patients benefit by avoiding birth control pill pretreatment and/or agonist pretreatment, and produce significantly better eggs on such antagonist protocols. Currently, however, this protocol should be considered investigational, as there are no randomized trials showing a benefit of antagonist protocols over the traditional approaches used for poor responders.

Antral follicular number	Antral follicles are small follicles (about 2 to 8 mm. in diameter) that we can see—and measure and count—with ultrasound. The antral follicle counts (along with female age) are, the in opinion of many IVF doctors, the best tool for estimating ovarian reserve, the expected response to ovarian stimulating drugs, and the best chance for successful pregnancy with IVF. Antral follicle counts are a good predictor of the number of mature follicles that will be stimulated in a woman's ovaries after injectable FSH medications are given. The number of eggs retrieved correlates with IVF success rates. 1. When there are an average (or high) number of antral follicles, usually there is a "good" response, with many mature follicles. Doctors get a good number of eggs at retrieval in these cases. Pregnancy rates are higher than average. 2. When there are few antral follicles, doctors tend to get a poor response, with few mature follicles. Cancellation of an IVF cycle is much more common when there is a low antral count. Pregnancy rates are lower, overall, in this group. The reduction in success rates is more pronounced in women over the age of thirty-five. 3. When the number of antral follicles is intermediate, the response is not as predictable. In most cases, the response is intermediate. However, doctors could also have either a low or a good response when the antral counts are intermediate. Pregnancy rates are pretty good, overall, in this group.
ART (assisted reproductive technology)	Assisted reproductive technology (ART) is a general term referring to methods used to achieve pregnancy by artificial or partially artificial means. It is the reproductive technology used primarily in infertility treatments.
Blastocyst transfer	A blastocyst is an embryo that has developed for five to six days after fertilization. With blastocyst transfer, embryos are cultured in the laboratory incubator to the blastocyst stage before they are transferred to the womb. At this time, one or two of the best quality blastocysts are selected and then implanted into the woman's womb. A blastocyst must successfully attach itself to the wall of the womb for a woman to become pregnant.
Cytoplasmic transfer	Still an experimental method in ART, this is a fertility technique whereby cytoplasm from a donor egg is injected into an egg with compromised mitochondria. The resulting egg is then fertilized with sperm and implanted in a womb, usually that of the woman who provided the recipient egg and nuclear DNA.

Depo Lupron protocol (also called Lupron Depot protocol)	Depo Lupron, or Lupron Depot (leuprolide acetate for depot suspension), a GnRH agonist, is a hormonal agent that significantly reduces estrogen levels. The medication works in two distinct phases. Phase one stimulates the ovaries, causing them to produce more estradiol, the most potent of the three estrogens produced by women. In phase two, the messenger hormones that tell the ovaries to produce estrogen decline dramatically. The resulting drop in estrogen causes women to experience menopause-like side effects. Lupron is an effective and medically accepted treatment for endometriosis. It also may be administered before assisted reproduction. In men, Lupron is used to treat advanced prostate cancer. It also may be used in children who are diagnosed with central precocious puberty (early puberty). Side Effects with Depo Lupron: Side effects that have been associated with the use of Depo Lupron frequently include hot flashes and night sweats, and less frequently, palpitations, syncope, and tachycardia. Other side effects include generalized pain, headaches, vaginitis, nausea/vomiting, fluid retention, weight gain, acne, hirsutism, joint pain, loss of sexual desire, depression, dizziness, nervousness, and breast changes, such as tenderness and pain.
DHEA	DHEA (dehydroepiandrosterone) is a hormone that is naturally made by the human body. It can be made in the laboratory from chemicals found in wild yam and soy. However, the human body cannot make DHEA from these chemicals, so simply eating wild yam or soy will not increase DHEA levels. DHEA supplementation is a relatively recent development for female infertility, used primarily in women with diminished ovarian reserve (DOR). Diminished ovarian reserve occurs either due to premature ovarian aging (POA) in younger women, or as a consequence of female aging. Introduced into fertility treatment by the Center for Human Reproduction (CHR) in 2004, DHEA supplementation has demonstrated remarkable results worldwide. Many women who had been advised by other fertility centers that their only chance of conception was with egg donation have still conceived with use of their own eggs. In the study on the effects of the supplement, Prof. Shulman found that women being treated for infertility who also received supplements of DHEA were three times more likely to conceive than women being treated without the additional drug. The results were published in *AYALA*, the journal of the Israeli Fertility Association.

	He and his fellow researchers conducted a study in which a control group of women received treatment for poor ovulation, and another group received the same treatment with the addition of the DHEA supplement. The latter group took 75 mg. of the supplement daily for forty days before starting fertility treatments, and continued for up to five months. Not only were women who combined infertility treatment with DHEA more likely to conceive, the researchers discovered, they were also more likely to experience a healthy pregnancy and delivery. Research showed that in the DHEA group, there was a 23 percent live birth rate, as opposed to a 4 percent rate in the control group.
Estradiol	Estradiol (E2 or 17β-estradiol) is a sex hormone. Estradiol is the predominant sex hormone present in females. It is also present in males, being produced as an active metabolic product of testosterone. It represents the major estrogen in humans. Estradiol has not only a critical impact on reproductive and sexual functioning, but also affects other organs, including the bones.
FSH	FSH stands for follicle stimulating hormone. This hormone is released by the anterior pituitary gland. In women, FSH stimulates production of eggs and a hormone called estradiol during the first half of the menstrual cycle. In men, FSH stimulates production of sperm. What does FSH hormone do? FSH is one of the most important hormones involved in the natural menstrual cycle, as well as in pharmacological (drug-induced) stimulation of the ovaries. It is the main hormone involved in producing mature eggs in the ovaries. FSH is the same hormone that is contained in the injectable gonadotropins used to produce multiple eggs for infertility treatment. FSH and luteinizing hormone (LH) act synergistically in reproduction. Quality of the eggs (oocytes) may also be impaired, as a 1989 study by Scott et al. of 758 IVF cycles showed a dramatic decline in implantation rates between high (> 25 mIU/mL) and low day 3 FSH (<15 mIU/mL) women, even though the ages of the women were equivalent between the two groups (mean age of thirty-five years). However, other studies show no association with elevated FSH levels and genetic quality of embryos after adjusting for age. The decline in quality was age related, not FSH related, as the younger women with high day 3 FSH levels had higher

	live birth rates than the older women with high FSH. There was no significant difference in genetic embryo quality between same aged women, regardless of FSH levels. A 2008 study concluded that diminished reserve did not affect the quality of oocytes, and any reduction in quality in diminished reserve of women was age related. One expert concluded: in young women with poor reserve, when eggs are obtained, they have near normal rates of implantation and pregnancy rates, but they are at high risk for IVF cancellation; if eggs are obtained, pregnancy rates are typically better than in older woman with normal reserve. However, if the FSH level is extremely elevated, these conclusions are likely not applicable.
Gonadotropins Gonadotropin-releasing hormone (GnRH) antagonists	Luteinizing hormone (LH) and follicle stimulating hormone (FSH) are called gonadotropins because they stimulate the gonads (in males, the testes; in females, the ovaries). They are not necessary for life, but they are essential for reproduction. These two hormones are secreted from cells in the anterior pituitary called gonadotrophs. Most gonadotrophs secrete only LH or FSH, but some appear to secrete both hormones. Are used to prevent premature ovulation in women undergoing ovarian stimulation as part of fertility treatment. It blocks the effects of gonadotropin-releasing hormone (GnRH). GnRH controls the secretion of *luteinizing hormone* (LH), a hormone that starts *ovulation* (release of an egg) during the menstrual cycle. GnRH antagonist allows the release of an egg to be controlled so it is released at the best time for pregnancy to occur.
hCG (also called Beta hCG)	The hormone human chorionic gonadotropin (better known as hCG) is produced during pregnancy. It is made by cells that form the placenta, which nourishes the egg after it has been fertilized and becomes attached to the uterine wall. Levels can first be detected by a blood test about eleven days after conception, and by a urine test about twelve to fourteen days after conception. In general, hCG levels will double every seventy-two hours. The level will reach its peak during the first eight to eleven weeks of pregnancy, and then it will decline and level off for the remainder of the pregnancy.
hCG injection (also called hCG trigger shot)	As ovulation will happen between 38 and 40 hours after a single hCG injection, procedures can be scheduled to take advantage of this time sequence, such as intrauterine insemination or sexual intercourse. Also, patients that undergo IVF, in general, receive hCG to trigger the ovulation process, but have an oocyte retrieval performed at about 34 to 36 hours after injection by, a few hours before the eggs actually would be released from the ovary.

ICSI	Intracytoplasmic sperm injection (ICSI, pronounced "eeksee" or "icksy") is an IVF procedure in which a single sperm is injected directly into an egg.
IUI	Intrauterine insemination (IUI) is the deposition of sperm into the cavity of the uterus using a fine plastic catheter at the time of ovulation. Before semen can be injected into the uterine cavity, the sperm must be "washed." "Sperm washing" and IUI are the same technology. Washing the sperm is the process of separating the sperm from the rest of the seminal fluid that makes up 95 percent of the volume of the ejaculate. This is done in the lab. It is the simplest of the reproductive technologies. Some of the other infertility treatments, such as or ICSI have a higher profile. Because of its simplicity, IUI is much more affordable, less invasive, and may be more effective overall, than the more intensive technologies. IUI is believed to double to triple the chance of pregnancy in a cycle over and above anything else that is being done. This is probably especially true if mild male factor infertility is present. It is also extremely important if hostile cervical mucus exists. Theoretically, IUI increases the chance of pregnancy by increasing the number of sperm entering the uterine cavity. We believe that when semen is ejaculated into the vagina that only 3 to 5 percent of the motile sperm navigate the cervical mucus to enter the uterine cavity. When sperm are washed, we can usually recover 20 to 50 percent of the moving sperm, and these can be placed in the uterine cavity, thus making ten times the number of sperm available at this level. The increased number of available sperm might not be the whole answer. IUI also involves detailed monitoring of the cycle using blood tests and ultrasound. Perhaps this precise monitoring also adds to the improved success.
IVF	In vitro fertilization (IVF) is the process by which egg cells are fertilized by sperm outside the womb (that is, in vitro). IVF is a major treatment in infertility when other methods of ART have failed. The process involves hormonally controlling the ovulatory process, removing ova (eggs) from the woman's ovaries, and letting sperm fertilize them in a fluid medium. The fertilized egg (zygote) is then transferred to the patient's uterus with the intent to establish a successful pregnancy. The first "test tube baby," Louise Brown, was born in 1978.

IVF closure/ IVF closure protocol	IVF closure is a term for the last IVF protocol with the woman's own eggs. In IVF jargon, it means closure cycle; last cycle to try before the decision is made to terminate IVF treatments with the woman's own eggs and turn to donor-egg protocol, donor-surrogate protocol, adoption, or the option to remain childless.
IVF protocol	In IVF jargon, protocol means hormonal treatment and monitoring of the patient (female) undergoing IVF. There are different types of protocols, depending on the type of hormonal stimulation, timing, and preparation. Types of IVF protocols mentioned in this book are: Long Lupron protocol Microflare protocol (short Lupron protocol) Agonist/antagonist protocol Depo Lupron or Lupron depot protocol Natural IVF protocol During an IVF cycle, certain medications are used to superovulate the ovaries in order to produce numerous of eggs. These medications may be given in a variety of combinations called protocols. In conventional IVF, two types of protocols are commonly used: the long protocol and the short protocol. The drugs used in both protocols are the same; however, the dosages and the period administered are different. The physician reviews the patient's records (woman's age, response to the medication, and outcome of previous attempts) and then determines which protocol will be used for the upcoming treatment cycle.
Laparoscopy	Laparoscopy is an operation performed in the abdomen or pelvis through small incisions (usually 0.5-1.5 cm) with the aid of a camera. It can either be used to inspect and diagnose a condition or to perform surgery. In gynecology, diagnostic laparoscopy may be used to inspect the outside of the uterus, ovaries, and fallopian tubes, for example, in the diagnosis female infertility.
Letrozole (Femara)	Letrozole (Femara) is a pill is used to promote ovulation and, therefore, pregnancy. It is believed to double the pregnancy rate per cycle and may be responsible for even greater improvements in women who are not ovulating.
LH	Luteinizing hormone (LH, also known as lutropin) is a hormone produced by the anterior pituitary gland. In females, an acute rise of LH, called the LH surge, triggers ovulation and development of the corpus luteum (cyst; temporary endocrine structure in female mammals that is involved in the production of relatively high levels of progesterone and moderate levels of estradiol and inhibin A).

Low (poor) responder	The term low/poor responder has been used to define women who require large doses of stimulation medications, and who make less than an optimal number of eggs. There is no uniform definition for low/poor responders, but many authors have used a cutoff of less than four mature oocytes at the time of hCG or a peak estradiol level of less than 500. Some women do not respond well to a flare protocol (or any other protocol) and are not able to develop enough follicles to allow a reasonable chance for pregnancy from IVF with their own eggs. These women are good candidates for IVF with donor eggs. Some fertility specialists believe that women who are low/poor responders might stimulate better if an antagonist protocol is used. This should be carefully studied in randomized controlled trials of previous low/poor responders to see whether it will be a viable alternative to other ovarian stimulation regimens for low/poor responders.
Long Lupron protocol	Long protocols (also called "down regulation" or "midluteal Lupron" protocols are the most commonly used IVF protocol in the US. Here are some other facts about this protocol: • Many IVF specialists think success rates are higher with this protocol (for most patients). • Lupron starts about seven days before the next expected period (called "midluteal timing"). • The FSH drug is usually started within the first two to seven days after the period begins. • The leuprolide acetate dose is often reduced when the FSH product is started. • The dose and brand name for the FSH product (e.g. Follistim, Gonal-F, Menopur) varies, according to the preferences of the physician and the patient's situation. • Most women get a starting dose of between 150 and 375 units of FSH product per day. • The dose is adjusted as the stimulation progresses.

Microflare protocol, flare protocol or short Lupron protocol	Flare Protocol, or Microflare for Poor Response Cases (also called Microdose flare, short Lupron, or short protocol).
	In this type of stimulation, the Lupron (or other GnRH agonist) is started on cycle day two in the same menstrual cycle that the eggs are planned to be retrieved, instead of starting it a week prior to the start of menses. Intention is to take advantage of an initial "flare-up" response of FSH and LH release from the woman's own pituitary gland, which usually occurs in the first three days of agonist administration. Continuing Lupron for more than three days temporarily suppresses the pituitary gland so that it has a low output of FSH and LH.
	The FSH product (e.g., Follistim, Gonal-F) is started on the following day (day three). The idea is that Lupron will stimulate release of a large amount of FSH (and LH) that will jump-start (flare-up) the follicles so that there might be better ovarian stimulation, with more mature follicles and more eggs for IVF.
	Birth control pills are usually given for the month before the flare so that there will not be a leftover cyst (corpus luteum) that could become reactivated by the high LH levels at the onset of the flare stimulation.
	An example of a microflare protocol is given below (there are variations on the theme):
	<ul><li>Birth control pills for one month.</li><li>Stop birth control pills; no meds for two days.</li><li>Start Lupron on the third pill-free day.</li><li>Start injections of the FSH product (once or twice daily) on the day after starting Lupron.</li><li>The Lupron is usually continued at the same dose until the hCG trigger shot is given.</li></ul>
	Some fertility specialists believe that lead follicle sizes with a flare stimulation should not be greater than about 17 to 19 mm, or pregnancy success rates may be reduced.
Ovulation	Ovulation is the process in a female's menstrual cycle by which a mature ovarian follicle ruptures and discharges an ovum (also known as an oocyte, female gamete, or casually, an egg). Ovulation also occurs in the estrous cycle of other female mammals, which differs in many fundamental ways from the menstrual cycle. The time immediately surrounding ovulation is referred to as the ovulatory phase or the periovulatory period.

Natural IVF protocol and natural low stimulation IVF protocol	As the name implies, natural cycle IVF uses no drugs to facilitate egg production. The cycles are not totally natural, because a single injection of hCG or Lupron is used to prepare the egg for retrieval. Occasionally an antagonist is used to prevent pre-mature ovulation and low dose of gonadotropins is used (natural low stimulation IVF protocol) Progesterone supplementation is still given after the egg retrieval. Candidates for natural cycle IVF include women with high FSH levels, because the addition of FSH usually does not affect ovaries already saturated with FSH, and women who make poor quality embryos with stimulation.
Progesterone	Progesterone is a hormone produced in the body which helps to regulate the menstrual cycle of women. Men also produce a small amount of this hormone, but it is less important to sexual maturity in men than is testosterone. Chemical forms of progesterone are widely used by women as part of birth control. The hormone's unique aspects tend to explain its effectiveness as a birth control method. In women, progesterone is produced just before ovulation in order to enhance the possibility of becoming pregnant. The rise in levels prior to ovulation increases the body temperature slightly; this creates more vaginal mucus, which makes sperm more likely to survive to reach and fertilize an egg; it also makes the uterus muscles less likely to contract. If a woman does become pregnant, main production of progesterone switches over to the developing placenta around the eighth week of pregnancy.
Secondary infertility	Term for a couple who already has a child or children conceived naturally, and has not been diagnosed with infertility, but who experiences prolonged difficulties trying to conceive more children.
Sperm motility	Sperm motility describes the ability of sperm to move properly toward an egg. This can also be thought of as the "quality" of the sperm, which is a factor in successful pregnancies, as opposed to the "quantity." Sperm that do not properly "swim," will not reach the egg in order to fertilize it.
Varicocele surgery	A varicocele is a network of tangled blood vessels (varicose veins) in the scrotum. It is a leading cause of male infertility, and it may also cause pain and atrophy (shrinkage) of the testicles. Many studies have shown that varicocele repair can improve semen analysis significantly, but there is no guarantee that any individual patient will experience a significant improvement. Pregnancy rates in infertile couples improve after varicocele repair by about 30 to 50 percent.

RESOURCES

Internet

The Internet links listed below (in alphabetical order) were resources for the preceding list of terms and definitions, including the explanations and descriptions of these terms. These Internet links contain various medical research reports, procedures, treatments, and articles related to ART.

http://humrep.oxfordjournals.org
http://womenshealth.about.com
http://www.abc.net.au
http://www.access.org
http://www.advancedfertility.com
http://www.americanpregnancy.org
http://www.arcfertility.com
http://www.bioedonline.org
http://www.centerforhumanreprod.com
http://www.drmalpani.com
http://www.havingbabies.com
http://www.hfea.gov.uk
http://www.highfsh.org
http://www.iaac.ca
http://www.ihr.com
http://www.infertility.about.com
http://www.infertilitybooks.com
http://www.ivfconnections.net
http://www.ivf.com

http://www.ivf-embryo.gr
http://www.ivfturkey.com
http://www.medbroadcast.com
http://www.mivf.com.au
http://www.obfocus.com
http://www.resolve.org
http://www.sciencedaily.com
http://www.sharedjourney.com
http://www.soft-infertility.com
http://www.treatmentabroad.net
http://www.varicoceles.com
http://www.webmd.com
http://www.wikipedia.com

Additional Books About Infertility

The books listed below (in alphabetical order by title) are ones that I recommend to anyone dealing with infertility.

Crossing the Moon—Paulette Bates Alden
Inconceivable—Julia Indichova
Inconceivable Conceptions: Psychological Aspects of Infertility and Reproductive Technology—Juliet Miller and Jane Haynes
The Infertility Book: A Comprehensive Medical & Emotional Guide—Carla Harkness
30 Something and the Clock is Ticking—Kasey Edwards
Infertility in the Male—Larry I. Lipshultz, Stuart S. Howards, and Craig S. Niederberger
Infertility in the Modern World: Present and Future Prospects (Biosocial Society Symposium Series)—Gillian R. Bentley and C.G. Nicholas Mascie-Tayler
The Infertility Survival Guide—Judith C. Daniluk and Margo Fluker
The Infertility Survival Handbook—Elizabeth Swire-Falker
Marginalized Reproduction: Ethnicity, Infertility, and Reproductive Technologies—Lorraine Culley, Nicky Hudson, and Floor van Rooij
Miracles Do Happen—Sandra Watson Rapley
Promise to Deliver—Rhonda Kanan

The Rollercoaster—Julia Masters
Surgery, Assisted Reproductive Technology, and Infertility: Diagnosis and Management of Problems in Gynecologic Reproductive Medicine—Gerard S. Letterie
Taking Charge of Your Fertility—Toni Weschler
Taking Charge of Your Infertility—edited by Kay Oke; written by the Counsellors at Melbourne IVF
This Too Shall Pass—Lori Durante Rardin
The Waiting Womb—Jill Sayre
Wanting Another Child—Harriet Fishman Simons
When Nature's Not Enough—Diana M. Olick

TEMPLATE TABLE FOR IVF PROTOCOL:								
Protocol:		No:	Type:					
Date:		Preparation for the protocol:						
My age:								
Clinic:								
Doctor:								

Cycle day	Date	Protocol day	Medications		Bloodwork		
					FSH	Estradiol	LH

Anastasia Sputnik © 2009/2010

	Ultrasound			Retreived eggs	Fertilized eggs	# of cells devided	Quality of eggs	Transferred embryos	New period
Left ovary	Right ovary	Endometrial lining							